D1446648

TESTED TO THE LIMIT

A Genocide Survivor's Story of Pain,
Resilience and Hope

CONSOLEE NISHIMWE

Edited by Bryan Black

BALBOA.
PRESS
A DIVISION OF HAY HOUSE

Library of Congress Control Number: 2012905480

Balboa Press books may be ordered through booksellers or by contacting:

Balboa Press
A Division of Hay House
1663 Liberty Drive
Bloomington, IN 47403
www.balboapress.com
1-(877) 407-4847

ISBN: 978-1-4525-4959-0 (e)
ISBN: 978-1-4525-4958-3 (sc)
ISBN: 978-1-4525-4960-6 (hc)

Because of the dynamic nature of the Internet, any web addresses or links contained in this book may have changed since publication and may no longer be valid. The views expressed in this work are solely those of the author and do not necessarily reflect the views of the publisher, and the publisher hereby disclaims any responsibility for them.

The author of this book does not dispense medical advice or prescribe the use of any technique as a form of treatment for physical, emotional, or medical problems without the advice of a physician, either directly or indirectly. The intent of the author is only to offer information of a general nature to help you in your quest for emotional and spiritual well-being. In the event you use any of the information in this book for yourself, which is your constitutional right, the author and the publisher assume no responsibility for your actions.

Any people depicted in stock imagery provided by Thinkstock are models, and such images are being used for illustrative purposes only. Certain stock imagery © Thinkstock.

Printed in the United States of America

Balboa Press rev. date: 06/25/2012

If there is one book you should read on the Rwandan Genocide, this is it. Tested to the Limit—A Rwandan Genocide Survivor's Story of Pain, Resilience and Hope is a riveting and courageous account from the perspective of a 14 year-old girl. It's a powerful story you will never forget.

—Francine LeFrak, Founder of Same Sky
and Award Winning Producer

That someone who survived such a horrific, life-altering experience as the Rwandan genocide could find the courage to share her story truly amazes me. But even more incredible is that Consolee Nishimwe refused to let the inhumane acts she suffered strip away her humanity, zest for life and positive outlook for a better future. After reading "Tested to the Limit," I am in awe of the unyielding strength and resilience of the human spirit to overcome against all odds.

—Kate Ferguson, Senior Editor,
POZ Magazine

"Tested to the Limit" is a courageous and beautifully crafted memoir that shows us how resilience and hope can triumph against overwhelming odds. By telling her personal story, Consolee Nishimwe advances the cause of human rights around the globe.

—Elizabeth Swart, PhD, MSW, Department of Sociology,
University of Central Florida

Consolee Nishimwe's story of resilience, perseverance and grace after surviving genocide, rape, and torture is a testament to the transformative power of unyielding faith and a commitment to love. Her inspiring narrative about compassionate courage and honest revelations about her spiritual path in the face of unthinkable adversity remind us that hope is eternal and miracles happen everyday.

—Jamia Wilson, Vice President of Programs,
Women's Media Center, New York

In reading "Tested to the Limit," one can either focus on the horror of a nation gone insane or on the bright spirit of a young girl, who, although temporarily damaged by unimaginable acts of cruelty, resists perpetuating the madness. Through ceaseless prayer, she proves, in this tale of hope and faith, what the Kabbalists declare, "that there is nowhere God is not." We learn that the darkest night can be filled with miracles. Thank you Consolee for telling us your story. Thank you for your brave heart. I bow low before you and those in this story whose humanity turned golden in those sunless days of Rwanda's genocide.

—Judith Garten, Spiritual Teacher and Counselor
and a Child of the Holocaust

*   *   *

To the loving memory of my father Andre Ngoga, my young brothers Philbert Nkusi, Pascal Muvara and Bon-Fils Abimana, to the hundreds of thousands who lost their lives in the 1994 genocide against Tutsis in Rwanda, and to the many survivors who are still struggling to overcome their trauma. For those who died, their ultimate sacrifice and the greatest memories of who they were throughout their lives will always be remembered, and for all my fellow survivors, your pain and suffering will be overcome through faith, hope and prayer.

*   *   *

"Let us always meet each other with a smile,
for a smile is the beginning of love."

Mother Teresa

★   ★   ★

CONTENTS

PREFACE

This autobiographical account is being told from my personal perspective and from my own recollection of events that occurred in my country which had a significant impact on my life. In some instances I have changed the names of persons who played an active role in the circumstances surrounding my life story, but I have taken great care to fairly and accurately recount my experiences in all instances I have described.

LIST OF ABBREVIATIONS

FAR   Armed Forces of Rwanda

MRND   National Revolutionary Movement for Development, political party of the Habyarimana regime.

POW   Prisoner of War

RPA   Rwandan Patriotic Army, military wing of RPF

RPF   Rwandan Patriotic Front, a political party formed by Tutsis in exile

RTLM   Radio Television Libre des Mille Collines, local radio station established prior to the 1994 genocide which propagated hate speech against Tutsis

INTRODUCTION

A Family's Anguish

It was April 15, and around 5 am that morning we found ourselves in the middle of some sorghum plantations near the Musogoro River hoping to move towards the area where we lived. While there we heard a large crowd of people not too far away chanting "Let's exterminate them . . . Let's exterminate them." Their voices were cold, menacing and full of hatred, and I felt thousands of chills running up and down my spine. I froze on the ground where I sat and my heart started to race, and all I could do was say to myself: "O God, help us . . . . God, please help us at this time." . . . We all immediately laid flat in the sorghum plantation and tightly held our breaths, hoping they would not find us. The killers kept chanting their extermination lines multiple times and running around eerily screaming as though toying with us, and shouting "Cut the sorghum trees . . . let's exterminate the cockroaches in there." The sound of their shrill voices so close to me echoed through my body. I felt like I could no longer breathe and that this could be our last day. The shouting became louder and closer and my heart exploded when I heard them shout: "Any Tutsi cockroaches hiding in there show your selves now and come out quickly before we find you and torture you to death!"

I felt like a thousand bolts of lightning had struck me and we all sat there on the ground trembling with fear. The faces of my dad and aunt turned white in a flash and I heard my mother whispering to us "keep praying within your hearts, God will be with us . . . if we have to die, let us all die together; . . . no matter what happens we will all be together." Aunt Kabazayire looked like she could no longer speak. I looked at my dad and could see clearly in his body language that he had given up. I started praying in my heart, focusing my prayers on him, and saying: "Oh Lord, please help my dad, don't allow anything bad to happen to him; I love him so much and want to keep having him with us."

The killers were almost upon us . . . . screaming and shouting like crazed wild animals, and chopping sorghum trees as they approached. I shuddered at the thought of those sharpened machetes slicing through our flesh and hacking through our bones and wished we could suddenly disappear . . . . We sheepishly emerged from the sorghum plantation, shaking uncontrollably with fear and holding on to each other as the killers closed in upon us . . .

We lost our dad and aunt that day, and three weeks later, my three young brothers aged 9 years, 7 years and 16 months old, were boldly taken away from us by killers, led away to our already destroyed home, murdered and dumped in our septic tank in full view of the public. Mere days later, I was forcibly abducted by a crazed killer armed with a sword, taken near our burnt out home, beaten and sexually assaulted.

For over three fateful months we faced many other insurmountable experiences, hiding from the killers from bush to bush and being turned away by people who we thought were friends. In the end, all the things we cherished were destroyed, and a number of other members of my family and extended family were murdered. Following the end of the genocide, I discovered that I had contracted HIV as a result of the sexual assault I had suffered during the mayhem.

My name is Consolee Nishimwe, and in the following eighteen chapters of this book I am going to take readers into my life journey from my childhood in Rwanda, and to describe some of my personal experiences during and after the 1994 genocide. I will also describe how I decided to live without anger or hatred towards those who had hurt me during that *period of darkness*" and how I continue to have a positive outlook on life despite my HIV status.

I hope that my story will inspire people all over the world to do their best to remain positive in their quest to overcome whatever difficulties life places in front of them.

PART I

A RUDE
AWAKENING

CHAPTER 1

A THOUSAND HILLS

My country Rwanda is a small but beautiful country in central Africa. It is often referred to as the land of the thousands hills due to the many gentle hills that can be found throughout. God created this serene land for us Rwandans and others to harmonize with each other and to enjoy in all its' splendor. I was born and raised in the western part of the country in Kibuye, District of Karongi. I spent my entire childhood in a small town called Rubengera which I grew to love so much from the time I got to know **"a wheat and a leaf green".** Kibuye is one of the more beautiful places in Rwanda. It is endowed with luscious green and hilly landscape interspersed between the glistening and enchanting Lake Kivu, which majestically winds its way through many parts of Kibuye, with several small inviting islands scattered within it. Like many other parts of Rwanda, Kibuye enjoys a very cool, fresh and moderate temperature throughout the year which many visitors find amazing.

I lived a happy childhood with good parents who were just regular primary school teachers but who were full of love and worked together to create the best for their family and community. I was also blessed to have loving siblings and relatives and good friends and neighbors with whom I shared the best of everything with love, joy and togetherness.

Growing up as a child in that environment and looking forward to a great future with everyone I loved, I never imagined that one day in a flash all that I was expecting to fulfill would be violently changed by such an insurmountable tragedy as Genocide.

For the first fourteen years of my life I grew up cherishing the fact that most of my close family members were around me, which was comforting and secure. Most of us were able to see each other almost on a daily basis, as we lived not too far away from each other. I still have fond memories of spending time with my paternal grandparents who lived directly across from our home and who we visited almost every day. I also enjoyed having fun with my cousins who lived less than two miles away. Since we lived close to the main road, they frequently passed near our house going to and from their homes. My maternal grandfather died before I was born. His wife, our grandmother, lived a little bit further about thirty minutes by foot from my house, but we still managed to see her regularly, mostly on weekends.

It was a great feeling, and regular visits between family, friends and neighbors to converse, exchange pleasantries, and update each other on issues whenever the opportunity arose, was part of our way of life. In our situation during that era, given the history of Rwanda from earlier times, family and friendship meant so much to us, and we as a people respected that and saw the extreme necessity to care for and look out for one another.

As I reflect on the closeness my family shared during my childhood days, I am convinced that there is no substitute for that feeling of hope, acceptance and unity which a sincere and caring family provides, especially when faced with difficult challenges in life. Such feeling goes deep within you and positively feeds your soul.

My mom Marie-Jeanne Mukamwiza and dad Andre Ngoga were born and raised in Kibuye where they lived all their lives. They were introduced to each other by a mutual friend who had a good relationship with both of them while they were all teenaged students attending different schools in the Kibuye area. Their 'chemistry' apparently clicked from the very first time they met, as after that first meeting in 1972 they became inseparable and started attending many events together in the area. Being awed by the kindness and pleasant spirit of my dad, I was curious to know what impressed my mom most about him when they first met. "Mom, please tell me . . . what made you fall in love with Dad?" I asked her one day. "My child, if you must know, I loved the way he 'rocked' as a goalkeeper," she laughingly replied. "That's it?"

I enquired. "No Cherie, your dad showed me his pure heart from the first time we met and that was sufficient."

I couldn't contain my glee after hearing her response and ran out of the room smiling shyly from ear to ear. I immediately went in search of my younger sister Jeanette to gossip with her about what Mom had just told me.

Mom was the fourth child in her family, having an older brother Alphonse, two older sisters Rose and Esperance, and a younger brother Vincent. She came from a truly respectable family who cared very much for one another. Mom was very focused on her education, and her determination to do well was strengthened by the great difficulties they had to endure to get an education in those days. She completed her secondary school with excellent grades, and earned her diploma in technical education and later became a teacher.

Mom and Dad belonged to different Christian religions but that did not get in the way of them developing a very close relationship. Mom's oldest sister Rose was a firm believer in the Catholic faith and had encouraged her to join the faith when she was in primary school. "The Catholic church will protect us from the troubles our people faced from the Hutus in 1959 and 1963," she quipped, as she sought to convince my mom.

"Do you really think so?" Mom childishly asked. "Of course, trust me on this" replied Aunt Rose. She must have been very convincing, as Mom promptly converted from Protestant to Catholicism and is still a believer up to today.

Dad was the eldest in his family of four boys and two girls. He and his siblings grew up as a close knit family with his mom Ancille Mukabaseka and dad Paul Ngirabanyiginya. Dad was a stickler for education and used every opportunity to insist upon us on how important education is for all of us. "You kids should consider yourselves fortunate to have access to education," he would often say. "Oh Dad, not another one of those lectures again," I joked with him one day. Taking me seriously, he quickly replied: "You should know that my parents never had a formal education and I was the first in the family to do so." I continued laughing as he replied, but to him this particular subject was no laughing matter. "My dear, education is so important to me that I have been making many sacrifices in order to send my younger siblings to school," he continued in earnest.

Dad liked to joke a lot, but seeing his eternal smile replaced by raised eyebrows and only a half smile, I had to concede and cut out the jokes.

Dad had excelled in high school and graduated with a first class diploma in teaching. His job as a teacher was very demanding but he was a very determined person and put his heart into everything he did. He was truly a strong believer in educating people. Many times he stayed late after school on his own time, giving additional lessons to kids who were having difficulties with their classes. I remember him also coming to the rescue of a young boy named Jackson in our neighborhood whose father had abandoned him and he was unable to pay his high school fees. Dad volunteered to pay the fees himself which allowed Jackson to continue classes and graduate from high school.

Dad also loved sports, and played soccer as the goalkeeper for his school, as well as the village team. Whenever he had the time he would practice his goalkeeping skills with other youths in the area. He was loved and admired by many people in the village because of his friendliness and good heart and the energy and passion he put into his soccer games.

Mom and Dad were engaged in a Rwandan traditional ceremony in early1977, and months later, in August of that year, they were married. They had five kids, with me being their first live birth. Mom told me amid a bit of sadness one day, that she had conceived with their first child shortly after their marriage, but had unfortunately lost that child at birth. She again conceived in late 1978, and on September 11, 1979 they were ecstatic when I became their first live birth! With a joyous smile on her face during that conversation, Mom said to me: "Cherie, when you were delivered as a live birth that day, it was such a great joy and comfort for me and your dad that we immediately decided to call you **Consolee, which means comfort, consolation**."

In 1982, three years after my birth, my sister Jeannette Ingabire became the new addition to the family. From her early childhood,

Jeanette was a loving and caring sister to me and my brothers, whose births subsequently followed hers. She was always willing to help out at home, making sure my little brothers were taken care of and contented. I loved asking her to help me do things because she never hesitated to help. She was a very quiet kid and didn't like to bother anyone. While I, as a child, loved to laugh and run around a lot, Jeanette was not like that; most of the time she would just watch me play and do her own stuff quietly. "Jeanette, let's go outside and play jump rope," I would sometimes beg her. "Oh, Macwa, I don't feel like it!" would be her usual reply. Mom or Dad would sometimes say to me: "Consolee, why can't you sit still and be quiet like your sister Jeanette?" and I'd reply "okay Mom, okay Dad, I will," and minutes later I'd be doing the same thing again.

I loved the fact that Jeanette and I understood each other so well even though we had quite different personalities. Whenever Mom gave us some tasks Jeanette would do them with a calm spirit and no complaints, while I'd be fretting with myself about the amount of work she had given us. Jeanette never liked talking much, and would always do things quietly and respectfully. She is my loving sister and best friend.

In 1985, when Jeanette was three years old, we were ecstatic when my first brother Philbert Nkusi was born. Philbert had a warm personality, was always in good spirits, and loved to smile. He was a handsome young boy with large charming eyes that sparkled whenever he wore his beaming smile. He loved to be around my mother and used to talk to her often. Sometimes at home he would be around her helping with some of the work she was doing. I remember every morning at school before we entered the classroom we had to line up to say the daily prayer and recite the national anthem. As a rule, whenever this was about to start Philbert would look in Mom's direction and smile at her and Mom would also look in his direction and smile back. I have never seen Philbert with a scowl on his face; he had a big heart and was always joyous and lively. "Consolee, your little brother Philbert is so friendly and cute!" my friends would sometimes tell me. He had a really touching personality and everyone felt his burning sincerity while around him. Even at a tender age, Philbert was already showing so much potential to become a great person in his community. When the genocide started he was in the third grade.

Two years after Philbert's birth, in 1987, my second brother Pascal Muvara was born. He was very funny, intelligent and energetic, and enjoyed doing stuff with my father. When he started school he hung around Dad all the time and bombarded him with many witty questions which were amazing for a child his age. Like Dad, he grew up liking sports and they used to listen to soccer games on the radio together. At age 5, Pascal knew the names of many of the players in the Africa Cup tournament, and already had his favorite teams. "Dad, it's Saturday, how about we go outside and play some soccer?" he would suggest as soon as it was bright outside. Pascal was also fond of gymnastics and was always practicing flips when he had the chance. He loved to be physically active, and was very creative in doing many things. Like my father, he was brilliant in almost every subject he studied and he amazed the family by how quickly he grasped knowledge. He was also a good artist and liked to sketch whatever he saw around him. His drawings were very impressive for his age and I believe he would have grown into an excellent artist. Pascal was in the second grade at the time of the genocide.

My baby brother Bon-Fils Abimana was born in 1993. He was the sweetest little boy and we all loved him so much during the short period he spent with us. He was a quiet and contented baby who did not cry too much. When my mother became pregnant with him we were surprised as we thought that she was finished with babies, since my second brother Pascal was about to enter the second grade. Bon-Fils was still a baby, approximately sixteen months old when the genocide of Tutsis began in Rwanda.

★　★　★

REFLECTIONS ON CHAPTER 1

Rwanda is my beautiful homeland which I will always love and hold dearly in my heart. God created me there and I will always remember and cherish it every single day that I live. Every part of Rwanda has great things to bring joy to its citizens and foreigners alike.

When the genocide took place in 1994, it destroyed so many things materially, spiritually and psychologically in that beautiful land and left scars which will take a very long time to heal. Despite all of this, I continually meditate and pray that what happened then will never happen again and that the next generation will take a different path and live a peaceful life full of love for each other.

Rwanda has been pulling itself out of the ruins of 1994 in great strides, and the next generation surely has a bright future to look forward to. May God always bless and protect our land and our people from ever reaching those unimaginable heights of hatred and ethnic discrimination again, and instead keep it flourishing in every way. Rwanda is, and always will be the land of the thousand beautiful hills.

CHAPTER 2

FAMILY VALUES

I grew up in a most loving household which I am so thankful to God for having given me. Mom and Dad both grew up being loved and cared for very much by their families and the values and teachings they imparted upon us during our childhood reflected many similarities from their own upbringing. Mom told us that her parents were very forward thinking people who gave her and her siblings a chance to do much more than they themselves had the opportunity to do in their early lives. They raised them with love and brought them close to one another and taught them the importance of family. Her father, Dismas Ruhago, who we never knew but fondly referred to as Grandpa Dismas, was asthmatic and died in 1974.

"Your Grandpa was a really great person who had loved us so much," Mom often told me as I was growing up. From what she spoke about him, I always wished that he had survived so that I could have had the opportunity to talk with, and question him, on so many things about his life, and get to know who he was in person. I truly feel that he would have enjoyed seeing his grand kids and show love to them as he did his children.

Mom and Dad were upstanding people in our small community, and they loved giving advice about school and life in general to youths in the area. They worked hard and put their heads together and built a humble dwelling which was comfortable enough for all of us.

From my early childhood I would feel the care and affection coming from my parents, especially Dad, who was fond of "his beloved little girl." He was very protective about me and made sure I was kept away from harm. I remember many evenings when he used to take me outside to play and laugh and to watch the moon and stars while Mom usually stayed inside the house doing other things. He was someone who liked to smile a lot and I think I inherited that trait from him. Mom would sometimes come out and look on, and on occasions would join us for a little while before returning to do other things in the house.

Being the first of their children, I basked in the outpouring of care and attention which they gave to me. When the time came for me to go to school, Dad was the one to take me there on that first day. It was fun but I was a bit apprehensive and needed him to stay with me throughout that day. Luckily for me, both he and Mom taught at my school. Dad and I maintained a close relationship and I always happily looked forward to walking to school with him, talking and smiling at each other with affection.

On weekends we used to spend a lot of fun time together as a family. Sometimes on Saturday afternoons Mom and Dad would get us all together in the living room where we would laugh, tell stories to each other and ask anything that came to mind. I used to come up with some weird and funny questions and they would be laughing all the time.

Even when we were having fun Mom seemed to always have work on her mind. "Sorry kids, I have to tend to my flower garden now, but you can continue playing with your dad," she would say after about an hour of fun. "But Mom . . . we just started to have fun with you," some of us would protest. Mom would smile to us and say: "Don't worry, when you grow up and have a family, you will understand," while rising to get her tools. She was passionate about growing beautiful beds of flowers of different shapes and felt happy to see them in full bloom and ready for making bouquets for the house.

"Dad, what can we do next?" I would sometimes ask after Mom's departure. That always seemed to be the opportunity for Dad to get us to do what he liked for a change. "You know what? We have talked and laughed a lot, so why don't we listen to the soccer game on the radio?" "Yes, let's do that," Pascal would shout before the rest of us could answer. We would sometimes fall asleep on Dad's stomach or he himself would fall asleep listening to the radio. When Mom was finished with her gardening she would come into the house and sit with us to relax while having a cup of tea. I enjoyed those happy times when we all had fun together.

Mom and Dad were obedient and thankful to God and they trained us the same way, always reminding us that "before you do anything else thank God for everything he does for you and before you go to sleep give yourself to him to guide you throughout the night and for other days to come." They also taught us to pray for everyone and obey and love everyone as we loved ourselves. I'm so grateful for the way our parents put their heads together to help us grow as loving children.

From as far back as I could remember, Mom would dress me nicely and send me to Dad's Protestant church service with him on most Sundays. Being Catholic, she stuck to her beliefs, but did not have a problem with us attending the Protestant church. She made sure that we knew how to pray and taught us to love God and Jesus with all our hearts. Prayer was a must in our home daily, and every evening before eating she would make us pray together, and after dinner we would sit together and sing gospel songs. My siblings and I loved singing together as it gave us a great feeling and helped us to bond better together.

Dad had an infectious smile, which was one of the good things we learned from him through our constant interaction together. In hindsight, I think he was unconsciously preparing us to cope with the tough challenges which were ahead in our lives. He brightened our spirits every single day with that joyous smile.

Dad loved to be next to Mom and they would often sit together outside whenever they finished their work, talking and laughing for hours on end. "Jeanette, look at the lovebirds holding hands and talking and smiling together; don't they look cute?" I would teasingly tell my sister at times. "Macwa, what if they hear you, are you crazy?" Jeanette would shyly respond.

Being a good cook, Mom would often cook some of Dad's favorite foods, which he looked forward to. She always made sure that he did not leave the house without eating something. I remember one day Dad was in a rush to get out the house and tried to sneak out quietly, but of course Mom caught him. Dad just laughed and Mom lovingly said to him: "Cheri, you should not leave without putting something in your stomach." At the same time, she shouted out to me: "Close the door Macwa, don't let your dad leave before he eats!"

As a child it was fun doing that, and I loved helping Mom make sure that Dad did not leave without having a bite of what she had made for him. I think he used to look forward to this, as on that occasion he laughingly told her: "I'll have a little bit Cheri; you know I love your cooking and won't leave without having a bite!" "Dad, you see I closed the door to stop you from leaving," I cut in. They both looked at me and laughed, and Mom replied: "Thanks Ma Fille Cherie for helping me catch your Dad!" It was always heartwarming to see them care so much for each other in such a fun and loving way.

Dad was someone I loved to be with whether at home or at school. He was my best friend and I wanted to be next to him every day. I often walked with him to school asking him questions about so many different things. He used to enjoy those conversations and would always tell me that he wanted me to learn lots of different things about our surroundings and life in general. He was very patient and knew how to respond in an effective way to anything I asked, and I felt free to question him. I spent a great deal of time with Dad talking, learning and laughing.

Mom and Dad taught us how to respect each other and others outside the family. The kind and loving way they used to speak to us impacted positively on me and my siblings and we learned to be as loving, polite, and pleasant as they were. They always looked forward to visits from family members and neighbors and they themselves made time to visit others as well. "A friend is one who visits," I remember Mom sometimes saying to us kids. Being curious youngsters, one day on a visit to Grandma Felicite, Jeanette and I asked her: Grandma, we visit you often, are we your friend? "Of course, you are my friends," replied Grandma Felicite with a hearty chuckle. "When people love others they visit them to show their friendship and to strengthen that love between them," she continued, with a serious look coming over her face. "Thanks for being our friend Grandma," we replied, blushing as we headed out the door. "Come back to visit soon," she replied, as we disappeared in the distance heading back home.

In Rwandan society like in many others, women are considered the heart of the house. They are responsible for nurturing their daughters' behaviors and growth by teaching them how to carry themselves with respect and to prepare them well for their future roles as wives and mothers. "You must learn to keep your room clean as a young girl growing up, Macwa" Mom would often say to me. "But Mom, I cleaned it last week and it is still clean," I would sometimes reply. "My dear, that would not work when you have a husband and kids, you know," she would often retort sternly.

I often felt that Mom used to overwork herself in doing things around the house. She was always on the go, tending to her flower garden, cooking dinner, or cleaning the house after getting home from work. To me, that was too much to follow. I was very young then and felt that I had a lot of time to learn those things.

Many times Mom would send me to buy foodstuff in the shop to offer to visitors to our home, or would sometimes cook for them and serve them as much as they can eat. Mom seemed to love doing this, and made me participate in what she was doing all the time, teaching me little by little. She also loved to "keep a clean scene" and that too was part of my teachings as I grew up. I enjoyed it, but sometimes as a kid I didn't feel it was necessary and would sometimes tell her: "Oh Mama that's too much cleanliness!" I used to think she was overdoing it, but as I grew older I learned to appreciate her wisdom of maintaining good personal hygiene and cleanliness of my surroundings.

I had wonderful grandparents, uncles, aunts, and cousins who made me feel loved and brought joy to me whenever I interacted with them. I think I was one of my relatives' most favorite kids and they showered me with so much affection and a sense of well being while growing up. My beloved aunt, Esperance, one of my few surviving relatives, provided much of that affection to me. She is a very calm and understanding person, and before the genocide she lived with Grandma Felicite and my cousin Chantal. She is very good at heart and kept the house spotlessly clean. I used to visit them regularly and she loved giving me and Chantal good advice and teaching us how to keep our surroundings clean and tidy. She always did it in a sweet way and we loved her for that.

Aunt Esperance was never married and had no kids of her own but she loved taking care of her nieces and nephews, and kids in the orphanage. She is the best aunt I have, and I am thankful that she is still alive. I talk to her regularly and we remind ourselves of the good times we had in the past. She is such a loving aunt and sometimes I like to tease her and make her laugh, and she enjoys those moments of laughter we share on the phone. She and my mother have been living together since the end of the genocide in 1994 and I am very happy for that, as they console and support each other all the time. They are very close as sisters and are also best friends to each other.

★   ★   ★

REFLECTIONS ON CHAPTER 2

The wonderful moments me and my family spent together as a wholesome group before the terrible genocide destroyed our family, could never be replaced. Our entire family circle including grandparents, aunts, uncles, cousins and in-laws was very closely knit and showed extreme care and interacted with love towards one another.

My parents showed love and affection for each other and knew how to care for our every need, and make us feel loved in their presence. They had great times together as a couple before their period of blissful marriage was unceremoniously cut short by the genocide.

I was young but I was able to understand how much my parents loved each other and how much they cared for our well being. I consider them as model parents and am really thankful and proud to call them my parents and my best friends. They made my days brighter and I still carry that great feeling in my heart even today.

A good and caring family is the foundation for shaping the character of children, and it is important that as parents and adults we never lose sight of our responsibilities to foster good attitudes and behaviors in their hearts and minds.

CHAPTER 3

TROUBLES AT SCHOOL

My parents taught me to always respect those whom I come into contact with and never do anything to offend others. They also taught me to apologize if I did something wrong or said something bad to someone else. I have never heard them say a word that denigrates someone else, and they never told me anything negative about ethnicity, or made me feel that I'm different from any other person. They wanted me to grow up respecting people, and constantly reminded me of how important that was for my upbringing. What happened next turned those teachings into utter confusion in my mind.

"Today before we do anything we will discuss ethnicity and find out who are Tutsis and who are Hutus in this class!" There was a hushed silence as many of the students looked at the teacher with confused looks on their faces. I was in my third grade class at the time and it would be the first occasion I would officially hear about ethnicity, as Ms. Fonseca shouted across the stillness of the room: "Those who belong to the Tutsi tribe should stand up so we can all know who they are, and then those who belong to the Hutu tribe should stand up after!"

As children, most of us didn't know the motive behind what our teacher was doing, but her body language and the sarcastic way in which she said it was not normal. "Tutsis, stand up first!" . . . . she shouted, as she waited with her pen and notepad. I and a large number of students did not move and remained seated. She looked around and pointed at me and a few other kids and said "You, you and you, stand up on Tutsis side! That's where you belong!" Me and the two other kids sheepishly stood up and joined the few others who were already standing, and I could see much discomfort on the faces of those of us standing. "You can sit now!" she said to us, after taking notes.

"Okay, now Hutus stand up!" she announced with an air of arrogance. The remainder of the class which was far greater in numbers, stood up and appeared much more at ease than we were. This made our group feel that something was not right with us, but we didn't know what it was. That day in class did not feel like any other day, and although not too much was said, the body language of both the teacher and the students who stood up last, somehow made us feel inferior and humiliated. I didn't know then that it was my official introduction to the strategy of ethnic division which had been in existence in Rwanda since long before my birth.

The funny feeling I had during that 'ethnic survey' stuck in my head and made me feel uncomfortable all day. I could not wait for classes to finish and to get home to tell my parents about it. Still shaken by the event, I feared talking to them about it while still at school. As soon as they got home that evening, I blurted out: "Mom, Dad, is something wrong with Tutsis?" "My child, what are you talking about?" Mom quickly responded. I looked at Dad who was very pensive, but he did not say anything.

"Today Ms. Fonseca made the class stand up in separate groups and told me I had to stand with Tutsis," I sobbed as I tried to explain. "The way it happened made me confused and uncomfortable, and I felt like something was wrong with us." Dad jumped to his feet and held me protectively around my shoulders and said: "Sit down my dear, and I'll explain a few things to you." Mom and Dad calmed me down by telling me I should not be worried about anything and that I would be okay, and that the two groups that Ms. Fonseca had asked to stand separately in class, were one people who have been living together for centuries. That worked pretty well, and when I went to school the next day I was able to play with other students as I usually did and did not worry much about what had happened the previous day. Even the other kids who were Hutus appeared to have forgotten about it and we played and had a great time together for the remainder of my time in third grade. Luckily, Ms. Fonseca never brought it up again.

Those times with my school friends were wonderful and I looked forward to going to class every day after that. I never had the slightest thought of being harmed by anyone. I thought all my teachers were wonderful people, but what some of them later did during the genocide proved how deadly wrong I was!

Every day when I got home I would tell my parents about the joy of being in school and how much I love my friends and all that we talked about in class, and would sometimes ask my parents if I can go and see them on the weekend. They were happy that we got along so well and encouraged me to keep on loving them as friends. It would be many years before I would come to know about some of the struggles which Tutsis went through earlier in my homeland.

As time went on, I continued to enjoy school and having good times with my classmates and did not pay much attention to the ethnic division the teacher had initiated in the classroom that day. I felt life was so good because of the fun I was having at school and the great life atmosphere we had at home with my parents and siblings. I believed that at my parents' job it would be the same, as they put so much effort into their work and I never saw them being mean to anyone. Being the child that I was, I did not realize that they were going through a difficult time at work because of their Tutsi identity.

From around 1990 when I started to become more aware of what was happening around me, I began to take notice of an escalation in anti-Tutsi rhetoric in the country. I gradually began to realize how public identification of Tutsis seemed to be a cue for extremist Hutus, irrespective of the status they held in the society, to discriminate against or mistreat them.

Sometime after the genocide of 1994, Mom and I were having conversations about life and other things I needed to know that they did not want me to know before, due to my tender age at the time. I really wanted to know full details of what they had experienced in their daily activities at work, so I continued to ask her about it. She related to me then, stories about how badly they were mistreated because of their ethnicity.

During one of our conversations one day, she said to me: "Cherie, what hurt me the most was to see how your dad was being mistreated at school, and I know how much he cared and dedicated himself to what he was doing as a teacher! As a male Tutsi, your father was a prime target for discrimination and ultimate extermination. It did not matter that he was a good and upstanding figure and was helping a lot of people in the area . . . He was Tutsi, and he was male—Period!"

Most times when we had these conversations we would both be in tears and it was always very painful for us, knowing in our hearts that we were being persecuted in the worst ways possible for simply being what God created us to be—Tutsis. It was more difficult for her to relive the pain again, as she had lived through decades of discrimination by people in authority, which they used as a precursor to the mass killings over the years of many innocent people who were massacred simply because of their ethnicity.

Mom continued to educate me over time on some of our history in the context of Rwanda's ethnic divide, when discrimination and genocide against Tutsis became institutionalized. She told me that from as early as 1959 mass killings of Tutsis began, and continued intermittently for decades without any form of censure or punishment being meted out to those responsible.

Discriminatory strategies such as an ethnic balance system for placement of children in schools was acutely disadvantageous to the minority Tutsi and Twa ethnic groups, and other strategies such as 'ethnic surveys' which I described earlier, aimed at identifying and humiliating those minorities at schools across the country. The long term results of such strategies became evident during the well planned and well executed genocide in 1994 which resulted in the slaughter of more than one million Tutsis and moderate Hutus, including hundreds of thousands of women and children.

Between 1959 and 1994, the targeting of Tutsis also resulted in millions of them being forced to flee the country to exile in neighboring countries, fearful for their lives and that of their families.

In relation to the direct victimization of some members of our family, Mom told me: "Back in the 1960's your Uncle Ladislas, then a teacher, was targeted by local leaders, constantly threatened and badly beaten, and with his life at risk, he fled the country following his discharge from hospital. He left to exile into Zaire and we did not hear from him for 34 years." Mom further explained that exiled relatives were fearful of communicating with their loved ones in the country, as those families would often be targeted as enemies of the country, and in many cases killed.

Mom also explained to me that in 1965 her eldest brother Alphonse suffered similar persecution by the authorities and vocal divisionists in the area who kept sending him threatening notes indicating that something was going to happen to him. He was very scared for his life, given the unclear fate of Uncle Ladislas which was still fresh in his mind. That same year he fled with the intention of exiling in neighboring Uganda, leaving his new wife and five month old son Jean Damascene behind, and was never heard of or seen again by the family.

Mom further related to me that in 1973 she and Aunt Esperance were both young adults still living with their parents, when they were threatened with death by extremist Hutus, forcing them to go into hiding for about three weeks. Their home and that of many other Tutsis in the area and other parts of the country were set on fire. She related that when the trouble started Grandpa Dismas told them: "Find a safe place to hide, I am not going anywhere! These are people I know and have lived with my entire life! I will face them and let's see what happens!" She further related that a group of angry Hutu extremists came while he sat in the yard, and ran into the house and set it on fire. They threatened to throw him into the fire and he defiantly told them to go ahead if their conscience allows them to.

Fortunately, in those times the hatred was not as extreme as it became in 1994, and they did not physically harm him. "Your Grandpa was amazed to see that the leader of the group was the pastor of his church who had baptized him a few years earlier," Mom recalled.

Mom and her family stayed in hiding for several weeks until the then Defense Minister Juvenal Habyarimana led a coup during which President Kayibanda was assassinated and Habyarimana took over the country, ending the genocide. Upon taking over, he told the nation it was time for peace! Little did they know then that the worst was yet to come!

In the years leading up to the 1994 genocide, Dad faced many difficulties in the workplace which Mom was aware of, being also a teacher there. One day she came home from work with my dad as usual and was overcome with emotion over the unfair treatment she had seen being meted out to him, and wanted to talk about it.

Seeing her unusual mood, I greeted her and went back to my room, not knowing what was happening. I strained my ears as I tried to listen through the semi closed door of my bedroom. "Cheri, I don't know what to do about what I see the principal doing to you and it is getting too much now!" Mom lamented in tears. "You do your best and you are a good man, and I think that if it continues you should consider changing your teaching profession and try something different!"

Mom started to cry really hard at that point and I saw Dad hold her in his arms and say to her with a calm and comforting voice: "Ma Cherie, don't get hurt, don't worry please! I will have to answer to God about what I did for those kids at school! Just let those who are mistreating me do whatever they want, as God will be the one to ask them about that," and added: "I love my work and the kids so much and I intend to keep doing as much as I can for them until God is ready for me to stop!" Those words had a calming effect on Mom and she said to Dad: "I love your strength and courage, I'm with you every step of the way Cheri!" to which Dad politely replied: "You energize me to do well, and your love and care strengthens me all the time!" From then on Mom grew emotionally stronger and remained positive despite all that was happening and they both kept supporting and comforting each other every day.

Despite all that was going on, my parents were still able to keep showing good attitudes and positive behaviors towards people around them. They kept serving as teachers and doing their work as best as they could and opening their hearts to people. There are so many Tutsis in the country who were really badly mistreated but never gave up on doing their best and being civil to others.

★   ★   ★

REFLECTIONS ON CHAPTER 3

I believe that discrimination supported by those in authority is one of the worst things leaders can do to their constituents, as it promotes deep divisions among different groups in a country, be it religious, ethnic, social class, or otherwise, and ultimately results in extreme levels of violence directed against the vulnerable groups.

Vulnerable groups in many parts of the world continue to be subjected to government supported discrimination even today, and we owe it to our future generations and ourselves to do our best to resist it at all costs and eliminate it once and for all!

CHAPTER 4

THE GLASS IS FULL

"The glass is full, we can't add more," was the Habyarimana regime's continuous response over the years to requests by a group of Tutsis in exile to return peacefully to the country. As a result, this group, many of whom were forced to exile since 1959 or were born to exiled Tutsis outside Rwanda, started efforts to return to the country by force. They formed themselves into a disciplined political group operating in exile under the banner of the Rwandan Patriotic Front (RPF), with a military wing called the Rwandan Patriotic Army (RPA).

Around the late 1980's the country had started to introduce a multi party system to compete with MRND, the single party formed under President Habyarimana. The new multi party system saw the evolution of several political parties whose radical agenda mirrored that of MRND and focused on propagating hatred against the Tutsis, openly calling on Hutus to hate them. I was too young then to differentiate much between the different parties, but I could see how the rhetoric from some of them started to quickly permeate through the country.

In late 1990 the RPF launched an attack against the Rwandan military from the Ugandan border and took control of a small part of Rwandan territory. This came amidst an outpouring of anti-Tutsi slogans and hate speech that was being directed at my ethnic group, which went on unabated for years. I was still in my first year in Junior High School in 1993 when the bad feelings I had in Ms. Fonseca's class years earlier, came back to me in a flash one day. "Hey, you evil Tutsi cockroaches are helping the Inkotanyi to attack our country," some Hutu classmates said to me and other Tutsis in the class that day. We became scared, as some of them were displaying bad emotions and hate, in addition to their words. Those of them who had displayed animosity and hatred to us appeared to have been effectively convinced about how bad we were, despite the good friendships we shared with them.

Not long after that first incident, I was again in class when a classmate who sat behind me in the classroom started punching me on the head, calling me "a little Tutsi cockroach." As a young girl happy to go to school and being friendly with all of my schoolmates, this radical shift in behavior took me by surprise. I became confused and started wondering to myself: "What's happening now?"

I felt very threatened by her since she was the mayor's niece and was behaving like she had the right to say or do anything bad to anyone whom she knew as a Tutsi. It was frightening to see how at such an early age she was already adopting the ideology of hatred against me and other Tutsis. Annie appeared to take pleasure in what she was doing, and over the next several weeks she continued to do and say offensive things to me and other Tutsi students. It was also confusing to see that no one was stopping her from what she was doing, probably because they were afraid that the mayor would chastise them.

Some of the other Hutu students in the class were also verbally abusing Tutsis, but at least they did not become physical. This went on for weeks and I wasn't defending myself or saying anything to her, thinking she would eventually stop, but the climate that existed at the time urged her and others who were following the extremists' plan, to escalate the strategy. I was truly scared and felt that I had to tell someone who could help me, but I did not want to burden my parents.

Our class teacher sometimes came to my house on weekends to help me in Math, so I decided to wait until he came one Saturday evening and approached him. "Mr. Laurent, I have a problem in class which I would like to discuss with you," I said to him as he sat down. Okay, what is it?" . . . he replied.

"You see, Annie keeps hitting me from behind and calling me names when you are not looking, and it's getting worse every day," I said to him.

Thinking that as my class teacher he would mediate in a proper way and speak to her about her behavior, he simply said to me: "I'll change her seat." I was disappointed that he was not going to talk to her, but at the same time I felt relieved that at least I would not be sitting close to her anymore. To my surprise, when we got to school the following Monday, Mr. Laurent never mentioned anything to Annie or the class, nor did he change my seat as he had promised to do.

As my teacher, I expected him to step up and do or say something about it and support me, because given what was happening in the country, I and other students were in danger. It became abundantly clear to me then, that I would have to tell my parents about what was happening. As we sat around the table having dinner that evening, I was my usual cheerful self, just waiting for the right moment to update Mom and Dad on what was going on. "Macwa, my dear, how was your day at school today?" Dad asked as he tasted his dessert. "I have a problem at school Dad, and my teacher is not doing anything about it," I replied sadly. "What . . . what is it my dear?" he asked in earnest. I explained the situation to Mom and Dad who were very upset and told me they would speak to my teacher to follow up on his promise to change my seat.

The next Saturday when Mr. Laurent came to my house Dad asked him about the situation and requested that I be moved to another seat as a first step. The following Monday he did change my seat, and I felt that at least during classes I could focus without expecting to be abused by that bully, and hopefully she would leave me alone outside of classes. Alas, that was not to be, as she insulted me at the first opportunity she got outside the class that day. After that, I tried to keep my distance from her as much as I possibly could.

Over the next months Annie's hatred towards me and other Tutsis became more and more obvious and I pitied the fact that she was growing up with such hatred in her heart. I often wondered to myself: "When Annie grows up, how would she be able to teach her own children to do the right thing? Would she tell them that they should love one group of people and hate the other without reason?" As for me, I was taught by my parents to love people despite who they are, so the thought of hating her or others never occurred to me. I just wanted her to change and be a friend because I never did anything wrong for her to hate me like this.

As I think about it now so many years later, I still feel disturbed, not so much about her behavior, but by the fact that grown people in positions of authority in the country and in homes like hers, were teaching innocent children **to hate without justification, instead of to love without reservation**. The poor child and many others like her were being taught to hate all of us just because we are Tutsis—no other reason.

Around that time while all this was unfolding at school, I remember regularly hearing on the local RTLM radio a rapid increase in its radical incitement of hatred and violence directed at Tutsis. Nothing broadcast on that radio station served as anything positive for the society—their main productions came by way of hate speeches of different forms and fashions which served to spread the ideology of hatred and to encourage Hutus to mistrust and dislike Tutsis. People all over the country were constantly listening to that station and it served to bolster what was already being propagated in many homes and schools. Extremist-leaning Hutus were easily influenced by it and allowed themselves to be blinded from the wisdom of acknowledging that it was wrong to hate with such intensity, people who had never done anything wrong to them.

During that period many Tutsis all over the country were being threatened and badly beaten and put in jail based on frivolous suspicions. I remember one night we were all in the house with our parents sitting at the table and having dinner. Pascal, who was five years old at the time, was asleep in the bedroom. That night we were happily talking and laughing as Dad was telling us some good stories, when we suddenly heard someone banging loudly on the door saying, "Police—Open up! Open the door now!"

His heart racing, Dad hurriedly ran to the door, not expecting something like this at that hour of the night! He used caution in opening the door, knowing what was happening to Tutsis. Of course all of us in the house were freaking out because of the noise the group created, and we were wondering what was going to happen. As Dad opened the door, a group of policemen rushed inside the house with guns and almost pushed him to the floor and shouted: "We are here to see the letters and the gun you have from the RPF Inkotanyi."

"I . . . . I don't have anything like that," Dad stammered, as they ordered him to throw all the documents he had in the house on the table. Dad protested that many of his documents were his school work but they did not care and forced him to read out loudly some of his personal letters which were among the documents.

While this was going on, they were throwing around mattresses and other stuff we had in the house. All of us kids and my mom were so afraid, wondering what would happen next. Pascal was still asleep inside and they went to his bed and shook him awake without caring that he is a young kid who was asleep. Mom held Pascal in her arms, while they made a lot of noise in a disrespectful way which also scared him.

"Pour those beans and rice on the floor!" came the harsh order from two policemen to me and our house helper. I became terrified, not knowing why those policemen were doing those things to us! After an hour of messing up the house and threatening us, they left everything scattered all over and insulted my parents calling them "cockroaches" and went away.

For a full week after that night, I kept recalling the anger and disrespect the Police had directed at us, and the threatening manner in which they had behaved. Those times were very frightening to so many Tutsis who were being persecuted in many different ways.

Not long after that episode, I remember one day as Dad and I got home from school I heard Mom immediately call him into their room with tension in her voice. Suspecting that something had happened, I strained my ears to listen to what they were talking about.

"Leonard was taken to jail with other Tutsis today and I am worried about what they are going to do to them," Mom sobbingly told Dad. "Which Leonard, is it your sister's husband? Oh, no, that cannot be right!" Dad muttered under his breath as he started to console her. Mom came out of the room shortly after and looked at me and my siblings and tearfully said to us: "Your uncle Leonard was taken to jail; pray for him so that he will be released and be able to go home. Pray that God will be with him!"

Uncle Leonard and others jailed with him were finally released after being made to suffer with little food for almost two weeks. On the day they were freed Mom and Dad took us to see him and we were happy that he had come home.

As the days went by, the hatred against Tutsis was getting worse, spurred on by the RTLM radio which kept spreading words of hatred and mistrust against the Tutsis. Few people across the country had the luxury of television, but most people had access to the local radio. Many Hutus had already accepted to follow the extremist ideology that was being propagated, as it continually called upon them to hate their Tutsi neighbors. There were some who were against that bad ideology, but were fearful that if they spoke out against it, they would be accused of supporting the enemy and their lives would also be in danger.

One day I was passing through the Gitikinini shopping area near our home and I realized that some dangerous looking gadgets of different kinds which I had not seen before were being made and sold. They were large long-handled wooden clubs studded with long nails at the top. They grabbed my attention as they looked so menacing! I was curious and wanted to know what their purpose was, but fearing what the owner would tell me, I did not ask. Seeing the way they were made with nails at the tips, my intuition told me that it could be a new type of weapon. It lingered in my thoughts a bit but I soon took it out of my mind and went to school.

A few years later during the 1994 genocide, those menacing clubs, together with machetes, the weapon of choice, and other different types of crudely made weapons were used by many Hutu extremists to murder Tutsis in the country. The thoughts that were haunting me from the very first time I had seen those clubs and the speed at which they were being bought by extremists in my area, finally became very clear—preparations had been in place for quite some time for mass killings of Tutsis.

★   ★   ★

REFLECTIONS ON CHAPTER 4

A serious social issue which affected us and which this chapter highlighted is the bad teachings of hatred some children received from their parents and other elders which manifested itself in their relationships with other children as they grew up in my country. It's a sad day when parents and other elders in society who should know better choose to teach hatred to kids, and cause those innocent children to act out on those teachings in obedience to them. Right thinking parents and grown-ups in general know that it is of great benefit to their children and to society to teach them love from an early age.

My wish for all people throughout the world is to help teach love and tolerance in each household as part of their daily duty, so as to enrich the hearts and souls of those around them with positive emotions and lasting consideration for each other, so we can all learn to get along in peace and harmony.

CHAPTER 5

FLEEING FROM HOME

"We don't want Tutsis around us, they are snakes! Kill them all and don't forget the small ones!" This was the type of hate speech that was being blasted from loudspeakers mounted on buses, pick-up trucks and other forms of motorized transport making the rounds in our village. I remember those times very well even though I was young, and it was very disturbing to hear the callous and open manner in which Hutu extremists were broadcasting and inciting the killing of masses of people who they didn't even know.

By about February 1994 the situation for Tutsis in the country was getting worse by the minute. In some areas scattered incidents of Tutsis being murdered without provocation, or disappearing without a trace started to occur. It began to increase in different areas of Rwanda as the Interahamwe and other militia groups were carrying out brazen killings of Tutsis in public view without any consequences.

By mid March 1994 it became extremely worrisome and got to the point where my parents started fearing for our safety at home, especially at night. The militias used to go to the homes of Tutsis or moderate Hutus at night and the following morning people would be found murdered in those homes. Even during the day people would be killed in their homes by these vicious groups and the authorities would never show up to investigate. Everyone was really scared of those groups because of how violent they were.

Seeing what was happening around us, my parents decided that we would not be staying at home at night, and started taking us every evening to spend the night at the home of a young Tutsi couple named Emmanuel and his wife Francoise. They lived within a Muslim community which did not display much hatred against Tutsis at that time. Of course every Tutsi in general began to fear for their lives at that point in time, given the near impossibility for them to escape from the country undetected.

From the day we started to overnight at the Muslim center, one of our house helpers left for her home, but the other one Marie Josee refused to leave and stayed with us. This worried Mom who tried to convince her to go to her family. "Things are getting bad, Marie Josee, and your parents may be worried about you being with us with all those threats around," Mom insisted. "Don't worry, Mama Jeanne, you are like a family to me. I want to stay with you no matter what happens!"

My parents did not further discourage Marie Josee who was adamant that she wanted to stay with us. It was truly amazing to see such a young girl voluntarily risking her life to be with others who were in danger. Marie-Josee is one of the Hutus whose refusal to hate stood out among the many others who had become so gullible. Mom and Dad appreciated her show of love and support but were still worried that she might get hurt with us.

"Mom, I am not happy that we have to leave our home at night, but I feel safer here in the Muslim community," I said to Mom as we walked to Emmanuel's home on the second night. "I feel the same Cherie! Let's pray that we remain safe from those crazy people," she replied as we entered the front door. Many other Tutsi families also sought refuge in that small community, as the Muslims there were not supportive of what was taking place in the area.

As the days slowly dragged on, we continued to hear personalities such as the well known singer Simon Bikindi singing songs of hatred against Tutsis on the RTLM radio airwaves. That radio station was sending hate messages of all sorts and encouraging the Hutus to "hate the cockroaches." There was high tension in the air and I didn't feel safe to go anywhere.

Dad's younger brother Athanase was home on Easter vacation, and one evening I saw him with my father standing near my grandparents' home talking and frantically looking across the street, apparently alarmed at what they were seeing. I could see fear on their faces, but I couldn't bring myself to ask what was going on. I did not know what next to expect from the situation but I was sure that it was not looking good for us. I thought about other members of my family and wondered where they were or what could have happened to them. A really sad feeling came over me, which spread over my entire body.

As a young girl who grew up being taught to respect everyone and love people unconditionally, I was now repeatedly hearing adults whom I respected, preaching hatred on national radio with a lot of anger and filled with such evil expressions. I felt like it was a terrible nightmare . . . What I was hearing and seeing was so unimaginable. Many times I would say to myself: "O Lord, what is this? . . . Why do we have to go through this? . . . . Is this going to be the end of the world?"

I remember looking at my father and reflecting on how good a person he is and how much he cares for people, and now he is being denied by some of these same people the right to live a normal life at his own home with his family. I also thought about the many other parents and grandparents who had done nothing wrong and were forced to flee from their own homes with their children to avoid being killed without reason. That was hurting my spirit and I just could not fathom the level of unscrupulousness that was being displayed by these people who had become so evil!

My heart was hurting so badly and it was clear that there was little or nothing we could do to stop what was happening except put our faith in God. My body became drained and I could not sit still or close my eyes and pray as I used to, so I spoke to God quietly in my heart telling him: "Lord, what's going on here? . . . I know that you love us so much, so I put all of us into your hands!" I was trying to avoid feeling frightened but it was not that easy. The feeling that something bad will happen to us couldn't get away from my mind, so I kept reciting that internal prayer over and over again.

Sometime during the evening of April 06 1994, we had already arrived at Emmanuel's home in the Muslim Center when Mom hurriedly handed me some money and said to me: "Macwa, I need you to go to the nuns' bakery to buy some bread! Buy a lot of bread, as I don't want you to be moving around so frequently, given what is happening!"

When I got to the shopping centre I saw soldiers standing at every corner armed with long guns, surrounding the center. I had never seen soldiers positioned like that in the area before, so I got scared and started to run to get to the nuns as quickly as I could. I arrived there out of breath and met Sister Ancille sitting at the bakery counter.

"Sister . . . . Sister Ancille, I . . . I'm in a rush! Mom asked me to get as much bread as I could carry and get back home quickly," I said to her, too afraid to even mention what I had seen on the road.

"Let me get you some fresh ones from the oven and let you go home," she replied. She then went to check the oven and came back and said to me: "They will be ready in a few more minutes, my dear." I was panicking as I wanted so badly to get home, but remembering what Mom had told me about getting enough bread, I had no choice but to wait. I stood there fidgeting and froze when Sister Ancille told me: "I'm going to get you something to drink while you are waiting," and headed towards the dispenser. "No, no thanks, I had some tea before I came!" I quickly replied.

It would be the first time I was refusing to have some tea with her while I waited, but I could not help it because my mind was set on getting home as fast as I could. A few minutes later she stood up and said to me: "Oh, great, they are ready now!" I was so happy to hear that and promptly stood up. I helped her put the bread into bags and started running home as fast as I could without looking back. In my haste I probably forgot to say good bye to her. While I was running my mind was racing and I kept thinking about how I was going to pass those soldiers at Gitikinini who looked so menacing and did not appear to be there to safeguard our well-being. When I reached Gitikinini I never looked at them and kept running fast until I reached Emmanuel's house.

When I got there my heart was still pounding and I told my parents what I had seen. They made a feeble attempt to calm me down, and I could see in their eyes and body language that they also were scared.

"Macwa . . . Macwa, thank God you got home quickly! Just after you left we heard that the plane carrying President Habyarimana was shot down and he was killed," Dad stammered. I freaked out on hearing that news, and felt so worried in my heart and wondered what was going to happen next. Mom and Dad also looked visibly scared, fearing that things would get worse because of the President's death.

The news was broadcast on the radio that President Habyarimana, as well as the President of Burundi were killed when the president's plane was shot down near the international airport in the capital Kigali. Immediately following the airing of this news, threats against Tutsis became much more amplified in our area, as we could hear people in the streets chanting anti-Tutsi sentiments more loudly than ever.

News started to spread that in Kigali, within minutes of the plane being shot down, thousands of Hutu extremists began mobilizing into groups armed with various types of weapons, and started attacking and killing Tutsis in their homes, in the streets, and anywhere else they could find them. We were already at the Muslim Center when the news broke, so we stayed indoors. In the meantime, broadcasts were being aired on the radio urging people all over the country to kill Tutsis wherever they could be found.

We laid low overnight and the next day the news spread that so many Tutsis were being killed in Kigali and other parts of the country. That morning we were standing outside Emmanuel's house and saw lots of people running on the streets, women with kids on their backs and men carrying stuff in their hands and on their heads, moving quickly and begging for protection. I got so worried looking at that huge crowd of people coming from different directions and thought aloud to myself: "What's happening now Dear God?" I was so confused and couldn't imagine what I was seeing. In my heart I had this huge fear and I actually felt weak, convinced that something was really wrong.

By this time many people from different regions in Mabanza Commune and neighboring areas were converging on the administration office to seek help, as they were being threatened and forced to flee from their homes which were being demolished by Hutu neighbors who had formed themselves into large gangs. Some were killed before they had time to escape and those who did escape thought they would get help from the local administration. The Mabanza communal office was situated near to where we were staying in the Muslim center.

Thousands of people displaced by the violence were there outside the offices with fear in their eyes, and the Mayor was encouraging them to stay there! There were many parents and children there who were suffering with no blankets and no food to eat. Some of our host's friends and family joined us in the house where we stayed. We kids were sleeping in the house during the night while the parents stayed awake sitting outside with other adults to see how things were going to turn out. In quick time there were so many of us staying in that house!

The Mayor and his assistants kept insisting that the people gathered outside the communal office should stay there, while the radio kept urging every Hutu to start working, meaning to start killing the Tutsis. Within those days that passed, Muslims who were protecting people in the community were being told by extremists that they had to give up on them, saying: "Those Tutsis must be killed, don't ever try to keep them in your homes!"

Broadcasts had by then started on the radio ordering that all the Tutsis in the country from young to old must be killed and their homes demolished. Some Muslims came to us where we were standing and said: "The government is giving orders that every Tutsi in the country must be searched for and killed wherever they are!" I became numb with fright on hearing them say this, and experienced a fear which I had never felt to such extremes before in my life. I was standing next to Mom and Dad and felt as though I was about to faint. It was so frightening to hear that the government decided to kill its own people who hadn't done anything wrong. I looked around and visualized how we are going to be killed without mercy and said to myself: "Oh Lord, protect us! Why are all these things happening to us?!!"

I was so terrified and couldn't feel my body anymore, and didn't know how to accept it in my head. There were about ten of us staying in that house at the time and everyone knew that orders had been given for us to be killed. No one could think of what we could do to save ourselves and the only thought that came to our minds was to echo the question: "How could this happen to us; what are we going to do?" Some of our young neighbors who were high school students came running into Emmanuel's house, out of breath. "We . . . we don't know what to do!!" . . . "Where can we hide?" they panted. I suddenly developed a fear that I cannot describe . . . . My body was overwhelmed and I couldn't breathe normally and was not sure whether I would be able to run.

The Mayor continued to lie to the many people gathered at the communal office telling them that they will be taken back home soon. In the meantime, the kids were crying out of hunger while the elderly among the group were not able to move from one place to another. It was very upsetting to see them in that kind of situation, although we ourselves were also in grave danger.

After about two days of telling the crowd camped outside the communal office to stay where they were, the then Mayor told them that they should go to the Kibuye stadium and stay there where they will be protected. Not knowing the Mayor's true intentions, many Tutsis headed to the stadium expecting to be protected as he said.

Thousands of people, young, old, mothers, fathers, grandparents, many of my friends and neighbors, family members, friends of my parents and others flocked to the stadium like the proverbial lambs being led to the slaughter. I remember seeing the long stream of people on the streets heading there and I felt so sad to see the distress on their faces. They were singing gospel songs and praising God along the route from the communal office to the Kibuye Stadium. One of the songs they were singing in Kinyarwanda stuck in my mind as it was a song we sang a lot in my church. "Help me Jesus, Help me, Help me, I have a body, Help me Jesus, because I face so many trials and tribulations!"

It was so sad to see my people crying in despair while singing praises to God. It was a sight I could never forget, and sad as it was, it was very inspiring to me. I spoke to God telling him: "Dear God, please make me and my parents strong like those people and help us overcome these difficulties!"

Looking at the extremely large group of Tutsis heading to the stadium, Mom and Dad were contemplating whether we should follow them or find another place to go. They were confused and went over the idea back and forth in their minds and eventually decided to follow the crowd to the stadium. Before leaving, they thought of going to a neighbor, Jackson, to ask him if he could take the keys of our house and safeguard our stuff in his house until things got better for us.

Jackson was pretty much our friend, as my Dad had taken care of him like a son and had paid for his secondary education when he was abandoned by his father. He lived just next door to our home and Dad thought him to be a great friend whom he can trust even in those extreme circumstances.

When we got to his house Dad told him: "Jackson, as you know things are getting worse for us by the minute and we don't know what's going to happen to us; if you can save some of the things we have in the house until we are able to return, that would be nice of you!"

"Don't worry Mr. Ngoga, I will save as much as I could for you and will do my best to keep your home safe," was Jackson's quick response.

Jackson appeared genuine while saying that to my parents but never mentioned anything about what he thought of the situation. Dad handed him the keys of the house and some photo albums which we had with us, but kept a small bag with some change of clothing for my baby brother and a few other small useful stuff we needed for him. For the rest of us we did not pack much as we could not risk being overburdened with a lot of stuff, not knowing how far we would have to walk and under what conditions.

We all said good bye and gave the keys to Jackson. As we were about to leave he said to us: "I hope things will get better and then you can come back home." What he was saying sounded sincere but his body language showed as though he knew deep down in his heart that chances of us returning were very slim.

We started running as fast as we could to meet Emmanuel and Francoise at their home and then to try to catch up with the other people who were on the way to the Kibuye Stadium. As we ran we could hear distressed moans and eerie screams of people up in the mountains. I remember that day clearly—it was around midday as we ran towards Emmanuel's home to meet him and his wife. By the time we got there, some of their Tutsi neighbors were frantically telling them . . . . "We must leave now and run fast to the stadium with the others! Homes are already being burnt and gangs have started to kill people!!" While talking to them, I looked up the hill and was shocked to see that our home, the home of my grandparents and the houses of some other Tutsi neighbors were on fire. On seeing this I screamed out: "Oh Lord, Papa, Mama, our home is burning!"

They looked up and saw many people running around destroying people's homes and screaming like they were crazy. On the other side of the hills other homes were also on fire and we could see many people screaming and scampering for safety while others armed with weapons were running after them. The atmosphere was just chaotic with different sounds of pain, despair and chants of jubilation all filling the air at the same time.

Seeing the level of carnage that was taking place, we had no time to wait around and lament. It was clear that we had to get away from the area fast. With all of us visibly shaken by what we had seen and heard, Dad held Bon-Fils in his arms and we all started running to catch up with the crowd headed to the stadium. Dad's sister Kabazayire and her 3 year old daughter Tuyisenge were among those who were running from their homes and we met them among the crowd on the street. Lots of people were also joining the large group heading to the stadium, but my parents started to become wary about going there, so we kept running along the road, not sure of what to do.

We arrived near a main road going towards the stadium, and could see a number of people in the area of the Kibilizi market, screaming while being attacked with machetes. Many of the attackers were also using those nail-studded clubs which I had been so curious about, and it then dawned on me that they were specially designed in preparation for the massacre of innocent people!" They nicknamed the club "Ntampongano Y'umwanzi" which means "no pity for our enemies."

Upon seeing the killings and hearing the loud screams of the innocent victims, Francoise became very scared and without warning she suddenly ran from the road and jumped into a large sorghum plantation and disappeared into the field. Her husband Emmanuel was also taken by surprise and started to scream: "Where did she go? . . . my wife will be killed! . . . I can't let her die alone!" He then quickly jumped into the sorghum plantation still screaming and frantically searching for her, and he also disappeared in the field. My parents became worried about them as they did not return to where we were. They were also worried about our fate, as we were all in the middle of a "nightmare." Mom and Dad pondered as to whether we should follow the crowd going to the stadium or find another place of refuge.

While we hesitated on the main street near Kibilizi market struggling with our thoughts as to what was best to do, some policemen in a car who were forcing the fleeing Tutsis to go to the stadium stopped the car near to us. Most of the occupants knew my parents very well. Mom and Dad also knew them, but their attitude towards us at that time belied their acquaintance with them. They looked at us from head to toe with such scorn and contempt, but did not say anything to us. Mom turned around and looked at them and said: "We are running from your people who want to kill us and here we are still meeting them everywhere; . . . you might as well just shoot us here right now instead of letting us run around to different places not knowing where to go!" The policeman closest to her looked at her without saying anything and laughed in a mocking and sarcastic way and they drove away.

We kept moving along the market road towards the stadium but for some reason my parents were still skeptical about going there. Mom suddenly had a thought of going to one of their Hutu friends, the Jean-Pierre's, who lived in a small village in Bubazi Sector, which was along that main road leading towards Kibuye City. Dad and Aunt Kabazayire agreed with her right away, and they told us kids that we would be going there instead of the stadium.

After walking for about an hour we were nearing their house when we came upon a huge crowd of Interahamwe wearing banana leaves around their waists and on their heads armed with machetes and clubs and chanting "death to Tutsi" slogans. Many of them were carrying a number of different items which we guessed were taken from Tutsis homes before they destroyed them. I remember how frightened

I became upon seeing them. They looked heinous and barbaric by the way they were behaving as they approached us and shouted: "Hey, you cockroaches give us what you have there!" and took away the small bags with the few belongings we had managed to take with us. I don't know where I found the courage to say to them: "Can you please leave us one?" . . . As I started to speak, one of them threatened to beat me with a machete so I immediately became quiet. They threatened us but didn't do us any physical harm. They appeared more preoccupied in taking our property at that point in time. We considered ourselves lucky that they had left us alive but were very traumatized by the encounter.

After they disappeared from sight, we ran straight to Jean-Pierre's home in Bubazi where they received us and immediately hid the ten of us in the ceiling of their home. The ten included Mom, Dad, Aunt Kabazayire, her daughter Tuyisenge, my sister, my three brothers, our babysitter Marie Josee and me. They distributed us in the ceilings of different rooms in the house and tried to give us something to eat up in there on that first day. While we were there we could hear many people running outside making lots of noises and chanting: "We need to exterminate all of those Tutsi cockroaches from young to old! . . . . Kill them big, kill them small! . . . Kill them all!" It was frightening to hear those things repeated over and over, given that we were already hiding like hunted animals, and wondering for how much longer this would go on. My siblings and I were very distressed. Jeanette and I kept asking each other: "Why couldn't we be at home having a normal life like Hutu kids? . . . . What did we do to make all those people want to kill us without mercy?"

While in the ceiling we were praying to God to help us and stop the vicious violence so that we could go back home even though we knew that our homes were already destroyed. That first experience of being crouched in the ceiling was very painful as we were not able to stretch our legs due to the cramped space; we were always on bent knees, and our backs were hurting so badly. We managed to sit on the wooden eaves of the ceiling space, but our backs still hurt. Four of us kids and Marie Josee were in the ceiling of the living room, where, through the little holes we could hear and see people coming in and out, and had to do our best to hold our breaths in order to avoid anyone discovering that we were there. Bon-Fils was with Mom and Dad in another ceiling in one of the bedrooms. They had a difficult time trying to keep him from crying. Being still a baby he was already overwhelmed by the commotion going on, added to the fact that he had to stay still in that cramped ceiling.

Sometimes I would cry and ask my young siblings: "Why are all these things happening to us?" and my 7 and 9 year old brothers would tell me: "Macwa, let us keep praying every single moment!" They somehow knew that things were really bad for us and we needed to pray constantly. At nights we were able to come out of the ceiling and go to see Mom and Dad for a brief period. They were all very scared, especially Dad who was worried about our safety. We kept telling them that we were afraid about what we were seeing and hearing while up in the ceiling, but they always comforted us by saying "God will be with us."

★ ★ ★

REFLECTIONS ON CHAPTER 5

Those first days of violence were very difficult for all of us who had to flee from our homes and join thousands on the streets with no fixed destination or safe haven to go to. There was so much fear among the Tutsi population who were being treated as though we were wild and dangerous animals that needed to be put to death at all costs.

People who have never been through such extremely threatening situations may never be able to fully comprehend the infinite fear that we experienced in those times, facing those terrible people with no means of defending ourselves. It is an experience I could never wish even for an enemy to go through.

I must pay tribute to our house help Marie Josee for the great courage and love that she showed us, and her determination to not allow herself to hate people who didn't do anything wrong to her or to society, and to love them just the way God created them. She chose to stay with us during our darkest hour, out of sheer love for her fellowmen.

CHAPTER 6

INTO THE BUSHES

"You will have to leave today! We don't want our home to be destroyed if the killers find you here!" Jean-Pierre said to Dad the day after we arrived. "Oh, no, can you please do us a favor and help us find another place where we can hide?" Mom and Dad begged. "If it's risky to have adults in the house, can you at least keep the children?" Mom added.

"Sorry, you have to find your own way; there is no way we can keep you beyond today—no further discussion!" was Jean-Pierre's terse reply. That was really not good for us to hear. We were already so scared of being outside and it was getting worse every day.

Jean-Pierre appeared so bitter and was not behaving nicely with us at all. It was very disheartening to Mom and Dad who had considered him as a close friend before. When the next day came it was time for us to leave. His adult son Julian and daughter Susan showed compassion for us and tried everything they could to convince him to help us. They went as far as suggesting to him that instead of us all leaving together we can leave Jeanette and Tuyisenge behind and if anyone asks who they were they would tell them that they are Colonel Junkhoo's kids staying with them on vacation.

The Colonel had kids of Jeanette's and Tusiyenge's age who lived in Kigali, so they believed it could work. Jean-Pierre was very stubborn and did not want to accept, but they begged him several times and he finally agreed that they could stay on the condition that everyone else must go and find somewhere to hide far away from their home.

By nightfall we had to leave, and Jeanette didn't want to stay there, while Tuyisenge was crying for her mother not to leave her. My parents and aunt convinced them both that we would see each other soon and we all tearfully hugged each other, not knowing whether we would ever see each other again. I was sad that Jeanette was going to stay but then again I thought she would be safer there. "I will see you Jeannette, pray all the time!" I said to her as we parted. She held Tuyisenges' hand and watched us leave the house looking very sad.

"Consolee, that top you are wearing is not sufficient to keep you warm while outdoors! . . . Wait a minute let me get you something warmer!" Susan said to me as we were about to leave. "This is one of my favorite sweaters but you can have it along with these few pieces of clothes for your little brothers. God be with you all."

I could see the sorrow on Susan's face as she turned around and went back into the house after I thanked her. We left in the dark of night to avoid the killers who we learned were all over looking for Tutsis to kill during the day. Julian led us through the backyard and through the bushes without passing on the street. When he reached near to a forest a fair distance away, he gave us a flashlight, said goodbye to us and headed back home. "Be quiet and careful going through those bushes," he cautioned as he disappeared into the darkness.

That night marked the beginning of an intense period of suffering and pain we were about to endure, not knowing where to go or who to turn to. It was like hell everywhere and our people were being killed at every turn. For us children that night was extremely dark, frightening, and definitely not recommended for our tender ages! As we made our entry into the dark forest, all of us kids were constantly falling down and at the same time trying to avoid branches and stones which was very difficult due to almost zero visibility. Dad was doing the best he could with the one flashlight we had to guide us all.

Had it been more pleasant circumstances we may have enjoyed the natural sounds being made around us by the frogs, crickets and animals in that dark forest near the Musogoro River. Truly, those frogs kept up a lively and harmonious rhythm, which I couldn't recall ever hearing before that night. As I kept hearing them, the thought of being attacked by snakes or other wild animals never crossed my mind. Even us kids who would normally be scared of lesser things, were all very quiet and tried to keep up with our parents as best we could to avoid being discovered by those misguided souls who were hunting us. I think those animals in the bushes also felt our pain, as they never bothered us.

As we got deeper into the forest it was getting tougher, as me and the other kids started to get tired and needed to lie down for a while. We had no choice but to lie down on the ground and partially cover ourselves with the little pieces of clothes Susan had given us. Luckily we had a few pieces of warm clothing as it was getting chilly.

As we lay on the cold, hard rocks, unable to sleep, Mom, Dad and Aunt Kabayazire sat next to us very worried, pondering as to where else we can go to hide before day breaks. I remember lying on that ground thinking to myself . . . . "We are children like any other children who at this ungodly hour would have been at their home sleeping in their beds, but look where we are now!" I felt hurt and prayed incessantly within my heart, and Mom was trying to do anything she could to make us strong. "Pray and talk to God every step of the way," she kept telling us. That night was filled with a lot of pain and thoughts about whether we would be able to survive until the next day.

"Sorry kids, we have to resume our journey although we don't know where it's going to take us!" Mom and Dad said to us after a while. "Okay Mom, we are ready!" I replied. We continued walking and they kept helping us to move a bit faster along that terrible dark trail filled with so many obstacles. Morning was approaching and we hoped that we could reach a residential area where some good soul would accept to hide us in their home before the killers emerge. Bon-Fils, who was only sixteen months old, was not crying or asking for anything to eat as we struggled through the forest, and Dad held him in his arms to keep him warm and prevent him from crying. For God's sake, he was just a baby and needed to be home like any other baby! It was getting closer to daybreak and we were still in those bushes trying to move quickly and find refuge somewhere, but the killers were starting to go into the bushes early to search for Tutsis.

It was then April 15, and around 5 am that morning we found ourselves in the middle of some sorghum plantations where we stopped to rest near the Musogoro River before trying to move towards the area where we lived. While there we suddenly heard a large crowd of people close by chanting "Let's exterminate them! . . . Let's exterminate them!" Their voices were cold, menacing and full of hatred, and I felt thousands of chills running up and down my spine. I froze on the ground where I sat and my heart started to race, and all I could do was say to my self: O God help us . . . . God, please help us at this time . . .

We all immediately laid flat in the sorghum plantation and tightly held our breaths, hoping they would not find us. The killers kept chanting their extermination lines multiple times and running around eerily screaming as though toying with us, and shouting "Cut the sorghum trees! . . . let's exterminate the cockroaches in there!!" The sound of their shrill voices so close to me echoed through my body. I felt like I could no longer breathe and that this could be our last day. The shouting became louder and closer and my heart exploded when I heard them shout: "Any Tutsi cockroaches hiding in there show your selves now and come out quickly before we find you and torture you to death!"

I felt like a thousand bolts of lightning had struck me and we all sat there on the ground trembling with fear. The faces of my dad and aunt turned white in a flash and I heard my mother whispering to us "keep praying within your hearts, God will be with us . . . if we have to die, let us all die together; no matter what happens we will all be together." Aunt Kabazayire looked like she could no longer speak. I looked at Dad and could see clearly in his body language that he had given up. I started praying in my heart, temporarily ignoring the fact that we were all in danger and focusing my prayers on him, saying: "Oh Lord, please help my dad, don't allow anything bad to happen to him. I love him so much and want to keep having him with us."

The killers were almost upon us . . . . screaming and shouting like crazed wild animals, and chopping sorghum trees as they approached. I shuddered at the thought of those sharpened machetes slicing through our flesh and hacking through our bones and wished we could suddenly disappear . . . . We sheepishly emerged from the sorghum plantation, shaking uncontrollably with fear and holding on to each other as the killers closed in upon us . . . Just before we emerged from the field Marie

Josee ran in the opposite direction and disappeared and we never knew what happened to her after that.

Over twenty killers wearing banana leaves and 'armed to the teeth' with machetes, clubs, spears and other crude weapons immediately circled around us, screaming and taunting us. They looked cruel and intimidating and Aunt Kabazayire lost her composure and suddenly darted away from us in an attempt to escape from the killers. Some of the killers immediately followed after her and killed her with machetes and clubs a short distance away. We could not bear to look at what they were doing to her, but my 7 year old brother Pascal had witnessed clearly how she was killed. There were also other people hiding in the plantation nearby whose screams we heard and believed that some of them were also killed. By the grace of God we were still there and the killers focused on Dad while the rest of us stood beside our mother, terrified from what they had done to Aunt Kabayazire and at how devilish they looked in their "costumes," armed with those menacing weapons.

The killers continued to surround us, talking loudly and threatening us with their weapons. It was such a frightful scene! Mom and Dad recognized some of them who they had either taught at school or knew very well in the area. "Don't do anything yet to the rest of them," one of the leaders shouted in a gruff voice. He then turned to Dad and said: "Give us some money and we will spare you." We were all still shaking uncontrollably, but relieved to hear him make that offer. Fortunately for us, Dad had about fifty thousand Rwandan francs which he carried in his pocket and they aggressively jumped on him and took the money. They greedily checked all his pockets further to see what else he had. As we stood there trembling, some of them took away the other stuff we had in our hands, but thankfully they left us there and went away without harming us.

Before we had time to leave the area we saw two guys lurking around the bushes and were not sure if they were part of the group or whether they were hanging around to see where we would be going. They approached us in an unthreatening manner, as if wanting to be friendly. Dad knew one of them who spoke to him in French, apparently not wanting the killers who could still be seen in the distance, to understand what he was saying to him.

"The militias are all around searching for Tutsis to kill and they are looking everywhere. Try to go through the bushes and go to your area and see whether you can find a place to hide!" he said to Dad. Seeing them talking to Dad and Mom in that friendly way, I thought they were going to help us, but that was not the case. They told us there is nothing else they could do except to pray for us, and then left.

The way they spoke made me feel that we had very little chance of survival. Nevertheless, we had to consider ourselves the luckiest at that moment to have not been killed there with my aunt and the others by that group. From what we had seen and experienced so far, it was clear that there would be little or no pity for any Tutsi found anywhere. We had no choice but to keep moving through those bushes scared to death, even in the brightness of day, with the killers searching all over and killing Tutsis in their wake.

Wherever we passed we were hearing the voices of killers searching and chanting their "extermination songs." We kept going towards our area through the bushes, sometimes going around in circles to avoid being caught. Dad was holding Bon-Fils, and we were all just following after him. After about one hour we arrived near the top of Rupango hill which was across the main road and also across from where we used to live, and we could see our burnt house in the distance. Just after reaching there some people saw us and started shouting loudly: "We found Ngoga and his family! Don't let them get any further!"

We kept moving faster, but they quickly followed close behind as we climbed the hill, trying to herd us between them. Mom and Dad kept looking back to help us move faster but we were getting tired as we climbed, and the noises the killers were making around us were unbearable. We managed to reach to the top of the hill and passed in front of the home of the municipal councilor named Nkiliyumwami, with the killers still closely behind us and screaming loudly "Don't let those cockroaches get away!"

Some of Nkiliyumwami's family and neighbors were sitting outside their homes watching what was happening and most of them were pretty much enjoying the sight of us being chased to be killed. Angelique, one of the councilor's daughters, recognized us and immediately grabbed Bon-Fils out of Dad's arms and shouted "follow me into the house quickly as fast as you can," as she ran quickly into her home. There was no other choice with the killers very close behind us, so we kept moving fast and were able to enter the house with Angelique. Knowing that men were priority targets, Dad did not enter the house with us but kept running towards another area known as Gihara Sector.

"Get Ngoga . . . Get Ngoga!! . . . Get that king cockroach!!" the killers shouted as dozens of them followed him. It was really terrifying to see those armed killers running after my father, and from the way the situation looked, he did not stand a chance!

Angelique and her mom Eva were very frightened and tried to find a place to hide us in their house. They quickly took us into a small room where we saw a young kid, Sandra, about six years old sitting near a small bed with large chop wounds on her head. Blood was still oozing from her head and face. She appeared to be hurting badly and was crying faintly. They told us that her mother had been killed and she was able to run into the house bleeding and they were trying to hide her. I felt sad looking at how badly Sandra was hurt and the pain she was in, and I thought that we were going to suffer a similar fate.

While in the room with Sandra, Eva told us that we should go into the ceiling because it was not safe to stay in that room. She further said that if the killers come to look for us she would tell them that we had left their house. She brought a ladder and we quickly climbed up into the ceiling. When we got up there we found a long flat piece of board which we used to sit on and Eva brought us a sheet and another piece of board.

The ceiling of that house was not as cramped as the one where we had first hid in Bubazi, so we were able to sit slightly more comfortably and Mom was able to sit and hold Bon-Fils on her lap. It was extremely hot up there and we were sweating profusely, but it was a pleasure compared to what we faced outside with those monsters who were hunting for us. I thank Eva and her daughter Angelique for doing what they did for us that day, for surely if they did not take us into their home when they did, we would have been killed right away. Eva took it upon herself to protect us without her husband's consent. He was not at home at the time, and that showed her deep sense of compassion, given the level of cruelty that was being exhibited by many of her tribal colleagues.

While in the ceiling, we were praying that Dad would be saved from those horrible people who had followed him, but remembering the fear and despair I had seen on his face while we were in the sorghum field in Bubazi, I couldn't reassure myself at all that he would survive. All I could do was keep being strong within myself and pray for his survival even though it was hard to think it was possible. Mom was very strong and was a source of strength to all of us while up there in the ceiling.

There was a large front yard outside Nkiliyumwami's home which was serving as a hangout where the killers would meet to celebrate and brag about how many Tutsis they had murdered. Some of them were providing beers to each other to reward themselves while they laughingly mentioned the names of people they had already killed and where they had found them hiding. Mom and I could easily hear their conversations and we suddenly heard raucous cheering and talking by an apparently new group which had joined those in the front yard.

"Ngoga has just been killed! . . . that Tutsi cockroach Ngoga, who just passed here, is now dead, he is no more! . . . . let's have some more drinks!!" they shouted loudly. When I heard that they had killed my dad, I felt like mindlessly getting out of the ceiling and walking on the street so they would kill me also. I felt like I had lost my mind and just couldn't believe that I had heard them say that they killed him . . . it was so overwhelming to hear, and I felt like my young heart was about to burst.

I could not hold back the flood of emotions which engulfed me at that moment . . . . My dad was my best friend and a great parent and I loved him so much and couldn't believe what those people were saying.

"Don't worry my child, your dad is in the heavens and those people didn't gain anything at all by doing that to him," Mom sobbed

47

uncontrollably as she held me tightly in her arms. "We might be next, so let's keep praying; . . . if something happens to us we will meet him in a good place," she quickly added.

My other siblings didn't follow what was being said outside . . . they were simply terrified by the noises the people were making. My heart felt so broken that day and I kept praying within and crying incessantly.

I was filled with a lot of emotional pain thinking about how I last saw my father being chased and how they must have tortured him before killing him. It was very difficult for me to accept the fact that I won't see him anymore. Mom kept encouraging me to pray, but at that moment I couldn't, as I was mad at those people. All I could do was to tell God to punish them in every prayer I was saying. The prayers became too complicated, and I could not come to terms with what those people were doing to us. The more I prayed, however, the closer I got to the point of saying within my heart that evil was working within them and I have to show God that I am not wishing them the same as they were doing to us. It was difficult but I never ceased to pray that whole day for God to help me.

★   ★   ★

REFLECTIONS ON CHAPTER 6

The memories of spending my childhood with my dad and other family members are the memories I cherish the most. My father and aunt will never be forgotten for all the love and pleasant memories they gave us. Like many families who lost their loved ones, their legacy and martyrdom will always be remembered and treasured in my lifetime and beyond.

It is unfortunate that at the time I needed him the most in my life, my dad was taken from us. He was the best example to me every single day and I am thankful to God to have at least allowed me to spend the first fourteen years of my life with him. Despite the fact that he is not here today, he has left an indelible impression in my heart for the great person he was, which comforts me whenever I think about him.

Some of those who were responsible for killing him have said that they did it because he was a Tutsi and Tutsis didn't have rights to live among them. It is so difficult to fathom what happened to the psyche of the millions of Hutu extremists in my country in the time leading up to, and during that fateful period of darkness which befell my country in 1994. How so many people could be so easily convinced to eliminate others who they had no issues with except for their God given ethnicity is something I can never come to terms with.

I could only hope and pray that the ideology of hatred no longer exists in their hearts or in the hearts of people in other parts of the world who choose to be so unkind to humankind.

My parents on their wedding day in 1977.

Back row from left to right are: Uncle Leonard (Deceased), Dad Andre
(Deceased), Mom Marie-Jeanne, Aunt Rose (Deceased), Parish Priest
Father Kanyabusozo (Deceased), Aunt Esperance, and Uncle Vincent
(Deceased).

Front row from left to right are: Cousin Jean-Damascene (Deceased),
Neighbor Christine (Sanani's sister), Cousin Aimable, Cousin Damascene
(Deceased), and relative Esperance (Deceased).

Mom holding my sister Jeanette, with me on her left in 1982.

PART II

SEEKING REFUGE

"To remain neutral in a situation of injustice is to be complicit in that injustice."

Desmond Tutu

★   ★   ★

CHAPTER 7

BACK AND FORTH

We were still in the ceiling the day Dad was killed, and in the evening Eva brought some food and water for us to drink, including some sorghum porridge for Bon-Fils who was very hungry. "Ngoga was killed today in Gihara Sector," she blurted out sadly as she handed Mom the food. "Be strong and pray that they don't find you up here," she added. We did not let on that Mom and I had heard everything that the killers had said, but our hearts were so pained that we could not contain our sorrow and burst into tears again when she confirmed his fateful demise.

After Eva left, Mom kept comforting us. It was extremely difficult for her also, but she showed such extraordinary strength in those difficult circumstances. I felt really bad for Bon-Fils as a baby in that situation. He had no clue as to why we were suffering. Many times he wanted to cry but we would rub his back to calm him and stop him from crying so as to avoid the killers from hearing us up there. It was the most difficult time for my mother to see her little kids sleeping on those hard boards. Sometimes I would look at her and she would turn her head and cry. As the eldest child I was more concerned with my siblings even though I myself was still a child, but I would listen to anything that was going on outside and talk about it with Mom and we would comfort each other. I was doing the best to comfort my siblings, telling them quietly that God will be with us.

As the days went by Eva came constantly to see how we were doing and to update Mom on what was going on outside. She and Angelique were the only ones who showed compassion for us at that time. They made sure to get food for us every evening during those first days in that ceiling, and were careful to avoid anyone seeing them come up to our hiding place.

After so many days of lying on those hard boards our bodies hurt so badly. It was difficult for Eva to find a safe time for us to come down and stretch, as the killers were constantly up and around. After four days in the ceiling she and Angelique were able to find time one day when no one else was at home, and they asked us to come down and lie on their bed for a couple of minutes. When we came down that day Angelique looked at me and said: "I'm very worried because my brother is also killing and has become so bad like many others out there; . . . because of how monstrous he has become, I'm sure if he sees you he might rape you and I don't know what else he can do to you afterwards; . . . . we will make sure you get back up there before he returns home and sees you!" When I heard that my heart started racing and I was very scared to stay any longer down there in the room.

I became so worried about what Angelique had said, that after stretching for only a couple of minutes in the room, I pleaded with Mom for us to go right back up into the ceiling. We were thankful that Angelique had alerted us and had made it clear that she was not in support of the barbaric behavior her brother and other extremists in the area were exhibiting. Even after getting back in the ceiling I was still terrified and said to my mother: "Mom, I'm so scared; what will we do if Angelique's brother finds us up here when Angelique and Eva are not at home?" Mom consoled me by saying "Cherie, don't worry, God will protect us from him." Despite the fact that Eva's husband and son were among the killers hunting Tutsis everywhere in the area, she and Angelique were very sympathetic to what was happening to us.

About three days later Eva came up to us and knelt in front of us crying. "I want to keep helping you but my husband is becoming vicious and horrible like everyone else; . . . I don't know what to do!" she wailed. "He is becoming like all those other killers, and is helping them so much; . . . he doesn't want you to stay here anymore and needs all of you to leave as soon as possible."

Eva later devised a plan for us to leave the house and try to hide outside in the bushes not too far away, and promised that she would bring us food whenever it was safe to do so. There were a lot of sorghum plantations and bushes behind her home where we could hide, but we did not trust that it would be safe, as killers were searching all over regularly and cutting down trees and plants that could afford concealment. We were left with no choice, however, so we had to give it a try.

She brought us food in the bushes from time to time and related to us that the mayor and his assistants were doing all they could to make sure that Tutsis were exterminated wherever they were found. "They are like monsters, and they have no pity at all and I'm really hurt about what I see everyday! . . . I feel bad seeing you this way as you are human beings too, but I will continue to do whatever I can to help you!" she said to us. Eva was one of the first Hutu that I had come across up to that time who appeared genuinely hurt about what her people were doing to us.

Eva had a little shack across from their home which they had built some time before and had allowed a villager named Bosco to live in. She related that he had some slight mental issues but was not violent and we could stay there at nights and return to the bushes to hide early on mornings. She warned us that this arrangement may not be easy because her husband or son could see us, and if that happens it would be difficult for her to protect us from them. We told her we would be careful and that evening she went to Bosco and told him of her plans but warned him that he must not say anything to anyone.

She gave us a grass mat and told us to go there that night. When we got there we spread the grass mat on the floor of a small room which all of us sat on and huddled together, as there was nothing else in the room. The room was a tight fit and the damp dirt floor a bit stony and hard, but was a little better than being in the ceiling where our backs hurt so badly.

"Get out of here! I don't want to be killed because of your little child crying," Bosco shouted at us the first time he heard Bon-Fils cry. We had to keep begging him to keep his voice down and be patient with us but he was going crazy every time he heard Bon-Fils' voice.

After that incident, whenever Bosco came to the shack he would say to us that he doesn't want to hear Bon-Fils' voice and would send us out and didn't care whether we would be killed. "I don't know why you are hiding; . . . . you don't deserve to have a life and you will all be exterminated anyway," he would tell us whenever he came from outside on the streets.

Mom did her best to reason with him by appealing to his conscience. "Don't think of us that way, because we are human beings like you and God sees everything," she said to him. "Don't be consumed by those wrongdoings; . . . make sure your mind is clear and love everyone because we are all created by God and no one is able to wipe out all that God has created!" she added. I was worried that he might reveal our presence to someone outside and cause the killers to find out that we are there. We were always scared of him because he was not that strong in his mind.

One day while hiding in the bushes we bumped into Julie, a Tutsi neighbor who was also trying to hide from the killers. We briefly spoke with her and she told us that she had heard that my cousin Chantal is alive and hiding in an unsafe environment close to one of the Interahamwe killers' meeting points! On hearing this news we became scared for her safety. She was the first family member whom we had heard of that was still alive at that time, and I prayed for her safety although we ourselves didn't know whether we were going to make it. Julie left after speaking to us and we kept hiding in the bushes throughout that day until evening.

Eva wasn't able to bring food for us during the day because of the extreme situation and we had to keep moving from place to place in the bush whenever we heard the killers nearby. As the situation worsened Eva came to see us less frequently at night and it was becoming very difficult for us without food or drink, especially Bon-Fils. As expected of a child his age he could not sustain his hunger and became impatient and kept crying and asking for food. This was very hurtful to Mom, yet she couldn't do anything because they were still searching all around and we had no choice but to stay concealed if we wanted to survive.

One day while in the bushes Bon-Fils was really hungry and cried a bit, and a young man who was taking some cows to the pasture heard him and came looking through the bushes and saw us. "I am going to tell the killers that you Tutsis are hiding here!" he shouted. "Please, please don't!" Mom and the rest of us begged. We continued to beg him until he finally accepted, and to our surprise he offered to go and get us some water to drink.

The guy left and came back some time later with a gallon of water which he gave to us and left without saying a word. It was a great relief to us that he had such a change of heart to get us water instead of reporting us to the killers. I saw that as an act of God's mercy to us that day, as we were so hungry and thirsty, having not had anything to eat or drink in almost two days. We were all thankful for that water especially Bon-Fils who became somewhat relieved in his stomach. After drinking some of it he laid down peacefully on my mother's chest.

After about ten days back and forth between the bushes and Bosco's shack, Mom felt that it was becoming too overwhelming for us and decided to ask Bosco if he could allow us to remain in the shack during the day also. She felt it was just a matter of time before the killers would find us in those bushes. Mom begged him if he could just lock us inside when he leaves on mornings as no one would think he was capable of hiding someone. It was very difficult for her to convince him but he eventually agreed. Although the ground was bare dirt and rocks and uncomfortable to sleep on, it felt like paradise compared to being outside in those bushes, and we felt lucky to be there.

It was still April 1994 drawing towards the end of the month, and we were still holed up in that small dark room of Bosco's little shack. One evening Eva came to see us and surprisingly brought Jeanette with her. When we saw them enter the house we were very shocked but happy that she was alive and wondered how Eva was able to find her. We all ran and hugged her, crying and thanking God that she was alive. She was also happy to see us, and sat down with us on that grass mat in the dark room. We asked her what happened with that family where we had left her and how did they allow her to leave. We also enquired about Tuyisenge and she told us that they had kept her.

After taking a few moments to settle down, Jeanette related her story to us. "I had no problem staying with that family after you left, but this morning their son Colonel Junkhoo came to visit and saw me there. He seemed to recognize me and asked his siblings who I was and they blurted out that I am Ngoga's daughter who they had decided to protect!" She added that the Colonel reacted by saying: "I can't believe one of Ngoga's family, a cockroach, is still alive and staying in this house!"

Poor Jeanette didn't know what he meant, as she couldn't clearly grasp the meaning of the term he had used to describe her, but she could tell that he was angry. She related that the Colonel's brother and sister became intimidated by his reaction and told him that all of us had stayed with them for a few days before they kicked us out. They also told him that they knew for sure that Ngoga, my dad, was killed the morning after we left their house, and we probably may have also been killed. After hearing this the Colonel was mad that they had not kicked her out with us, and he angrily told them: "She has to leave here right away, and I don't care what happens to her; they are all going to be killed anyway!" Jeanette related that she was very afraid when she heard him say that and wondered why he wanted her to die!

The Colonel was giving orders, and his relatives went to her and told her that she had to go to her home. Almost in tears, she replied to them: "I don't have a home anymore; . . . my home is destroyed and I don't know where to go; . . . I don't know where my parents and siblings are!" to which they callously replied: "You have to go and find them and whatever happens to you we hope it happens away from here!"

Jeanette was still a little girl and didn't know what to do or why these things were happening to us. It was broad daylight when she left their house and she wandered along the main road passing many killers armed with machetes and clubs and other people coming from the Kibilizi market. Fortunately, no one paid attention to her, probably thinking that a Tutsi had to be crazy to walk in the open like that knowing what was happening to them.

Jeanette told us that she didn't care what was going to happen to her, having heard that Dad was killed and thought that we all might have also been killed, and didn't know what else to do. She was just walking and waiting to see what was going to happen. As she kept walking along the street, Nathalie, a Hutu neighbor saw her and quickly ran to her and pulled her off the road saying: "Oh my God, Ngoga's child you are on the street at this time of the day in the middle of the killers; . . . . they have no mercy at all; . . . if they had recognized you they would have killed you!" Nathalie was scared that Jeanette might be killed but was afraid to keep her even though she had taken her off the street.

All news relating to the demise of Tutsis were quickly spread to villagers every day, so Nathalie had heard that we were seen going to Nkiliyumwami's house the day my father was chased and killed, but didn't know if we were still there. She, however, decided to see Eva and tell her that she had found Jeanette in the street but could not keep her at her home. Before she could say anything further Eva told her right away that she would hide her, and insisted upon Nathalie that she must never mention that we were hiding in her house. Following that conversation, Nathalie brought Jeanette to Eva early that evening, and after darkness fell, Eva brought her to us in that small shack.

After hearing that story we were so thankful to that goodly Hutu neighbor who had rescued my sister. It showed to us that despite the mad killing frenzy by so many Hutus who had suddenly become extreme, there were still some who were good at heart and refused to be influenced by what the majority were doing to us Tutsis.

On the other hand, it was difficult to accept how Colonel Junkhoo who had children of his own, would expose a kid of Jeanette's age to almost certain death. How heartless so many of them had become even to children! I was more disappointed than angry at the Colonel for what he had done, and convinced myself that he would have to answer for that on judgment day. I felt that I didn't have the space in my heart to carry hatred for him and the thousands of others who were making our lives a living hell.

After hearing what had happened, we prayed a lot and thanked God for protecting Jeanette from those killers in the streets which were so dangerous at that time.

★   ★   ★

REFLECTIONS ON CHAPTER 7

It was refreshing to see that at least there were some of our Hutu neighbors who showed some compassion for our situation. It was such a sharp contrast that Eva and her daughter Angelique were risking their lives to care for our safety, while her husband and son were leading the charge to kill other Tutsis.

The most powerful highlight of this chapter was our experience of God's divine intervention at the time we were discovered in the bushes and threatened that our presence would be reported to the killers. God showed his hand to us that day by changing the mind of that unidentified young man who voluntarily turned around and brought us water after initially threatening to report us to the killers.

CHAPTER 8

CHANGES IN ONCE-FRIENDLY HEARTS

The dark silhouette of an Interahamwe killer with his hand upraised, suddenly appeared in the doorway to our 'room' in the shack as we sat there one evening. We cowered in fear, expecting to be chopped by a machete, as Mom shouted: "Don't kill us; please don't kill us." We were relieved to hear the quick reply "Miss Jeanne, is that you? Don't worry, I'm your neighbor Innocent, I'm not a killer."

We were amazed that Innocent had immediately recognized my mom's voice as she pleaded, and as he spoke, we also promptly recognized his. "Innocent, are you okay?' Mom whispered as she looked at the bloodied cloth wrapped around his right hand. "No, Miss Jeanne, my hand is in bad shape," he whispered quietly, wincing in pain. "How did you find us here?" Mom enquired with concern. "I was attacked but escaped from the killers and hid from them, and stumbled through the bushes for many days until I came upon this deserted shack, so I ran in through the half open door," he replied.

Innocent was very scared and clearly in pain, and sat down on the floor not very far from us and continued to relate his story. "I was at the Kibuye stadium with thousands of other Tutsis believing the mayor that we would be protected there, but after it filled up with our people, soldiers threw grenades and started shooting incessantly at all of us who were inside . . . . My hand almost got blown off but I escaped through the bushes where I have been hiding since," he lamented.

He related to us that thousands of people, some of whom we knew, were killed there, and also many others who had sought refuge in the

Saint Jean church were attacked and killed. "Dead bodies were strewn everywhere, but I cannot say if any of your family members were among those killed," he responded sadly to a query from Mom. The wound on Innocent's hand was in very bad shape and there was nothing we could do to help him.

"Whose male voice is that I hear in there with you?" Bosco chided as he rushed into the room a few minutes later. "It's our Tutsi neighbor who is badly injured and needs help Bosco," Mom replied. "I don't care, he has to leave immediately," said Bosco, without any show of pity. Innocent immediately rose to his feet and told Bosco that it was okay and that he would leave. "I don't know whether we're going to see each other again on this earth," he muttered to us as he quickly said goodbye and disappeared into the darkness. We sat there quietly, sad to see him leave and I kept thinking of the pain he was in and wondering how he would survive without medical help and a place to hide.

The next day Bosco came home and told us: "That man who was here last night was found hiding in the bushes not too far from here and he tried to run but his attackers caught up with him and killed him right away!" From the amused way in which he spoke, it was obvious that he was not disturbed by what had happened to Innocent; he narrated the story as though it was an animal hunt. It pained me to see how indifferent our people had become about the killing of Tutsis as if we were vermin who had to be gotten rid of at all costs.

Later that evening we were sitting on the grass mat in that dark room praying together and making sure Bon-Fils does not cry. We heard Eva coming into the shack as usual, but what we didn't know was that evening was going to be different. With tears streaming down her face, she came in and sat next to Mom. "Jeanne, I want to keep helping you . . . but . . . but . . . it's getting too difficult for me . . . . and they are killing like crazy everywhere," she sighed as she spoke. "It's difficult for me to tell you to leave . . . but I won't be able to hide you any longer . . . they are searching everywhere and I don't want you to be killed here!"

That night Eva didn't stay as long as she usually did and said good bye to us and told us that she will pray for us every single day. We agreed to leave even though we didn't know where to go. Mom started wondering where we could go from there. The area where we were was near to two main gathering places of the Interahamwe groups, where many of them would either stop outside Eva's home after each day's killing tasks to drink beers and talk about who and how many they have killed, or go to the Mayor's house which was also nearby, to do the same.

Mom thought deeply about our options for quite some time, at the same time waiting for darkness to fall before we leave. She thought about trying to go to the area where she grew up as a child which was not very far from where we were, with the hope that there were still some people left who had the heart and mind to help us hide. We couldn't guess who we could count on because so many people had become merciless. We had no choice but to try, as we had to leave that night. Mom slung Bon-Fils across her back and secured him with a cloth as the rest of us followed her out of the house and into the cold dark night . . .

As we waded through the bushes it was so dark and the frogs and crickets were singing all around us. It was the rainy season, and not long after we left there was a sudden downpour of rain which made our trek through the bushes even more treacherous. Many killers were operating roadblocks all over and we could hear them making a lot of noise at Gitikinini shopping center and near the Rubengera High School. We did our best to avoid getting close to those areas because it was going to be the end of us.

As we walked through the darkness, I kept slipping in the mud. I was weak through lack of food and fell down several times. Poor Mom had to help me get back on my feet with Bon-Fils on her back. Jeanette and my two young brothers somehow managed to move on their own, and whenever they fell they would quickly get up and keep moving on. The rain continued for most of that night and we became soaked as Mom struggled to find a good path for us to follow, she herself falling down many times.

That night was extremely challenging for us. With only rubber flip flops on our feet, we constantly had to take them off because of the mud and stones, and walking barefooted caused our little feet to become bruised and painful as we stepped on them over and over. We kept going until we arrived to the home of a friend and neighbor of Grandma Felicite, confident that they would have pity on us since we knew them as good prayerful people.

As we stood outside the door we could hear a large group of people praying and singing inside. We never hesitated and knocked on the door until they heard us. After a few minutes the singing finally stopped and someone peeped through the window but no one opened the door. "Don't come here Jeanne! We don't want to be killed with you!" Josiane, the woman of the house, shouted from inside. "We are getting ready for the Sabbath, please go away!" she added.

"Please, I have the kids . . . please let them get out of the rain and breathe for a little while!" Mom pleaded. There was a brief silence while the door remained closed, and the singing and worshiping resumed unashamedly.

We felt dejected and stood outside for a while as Mom pondered about what to do. We were about to re-enter the bushes when we saw a guy walking around in that dark night. "I see some Tutsis around here; come very quickly!" shouted the guy as he called the attention of others to us.

Still shouting, he ran towards us and as he got closer we realized it was Jean-Paul, a neighbor of my Grandma Felicite. Jean-Paul suddenly pulled up when he recognized who we were. "Oh, Ms. Jeanne it's you; . . . I can't call the killers for you, you have been good to me!" he said apologetically, and quickly turned around and shouted: "Don't bother, I made a mistake; . . . it was some cows walking through the bushes!" Jean-Paul then quickly told us: "Don't ever try to walk in the streets, especially near Gitikinini and the high school; . . . avoid them as much as you could, because that's where all the killers are staying and having roadblocks," and added: "I'm not sure that you'll be able to find a hiding place . . . and I'm sorry that I myself can't help you!"

"Do you think it's safe to try the home of Jules who is a family friend and former colleague of Ngoga?" Mom asked him enquiringly.

"Don't even think of going there . . . that home is frequented by killers who spend a lot of time there; . . . if they see you it's over with you!"

By this time some people had already started to come out of their homes and Jean-Paul walked towards them while we disappeared through the bushes into the darkness. It was now becoming abundantly clear to us that there were very few people around who were not involved in supporting or carrying out the genocide. Nevertheless, we had to keep moving, and to keep ourselves strong all we could do was pray for God's continued protection every step of the way. We were dripping wet and cold, hungry, and very tired, with no place of refuge, and daylight was fast approaching . . . .

Faced with limited options, Mom decided to try the home of a family that were very good friends to us and lived across from the Rubengera High School. Although they lived very close to a major Interahamwe base, she felt they would not turn their backs on us because of the relationship we shared with them.

Around 5 am that morning we arrived there and approached the house from behind and knocked on the back door. No one answered, but we could hear people murmuring inside the house talking to each other in undertones. After about three minutes, Leon, the man of the house asked: "Who's there at my door?" "Leon it's Marie-Jeanne!" Mom replied to him. "Oh, that's you Marie—Jeanne!" he responded. We then heard him murmuring again with his wife but we could not hear clearly what they were talking about. "Would you help and hide us please? We don't have anywhere else to go!" Mom said pleadingly. He then spoke to us softly from inside the house urging us to leave, but we didn't budge, hoping that he would change his mind.

At first it didn't seem like he was serious about telling us to leave, but as we kept listening we could hear him arguing inside under his breath with his wife Lucille. Lucille never said a word to us, although Mom was her good friend. We didn't know what exactly they were saying to each other but we felt they were too close to us as friends to turn us away.

After a few minutes, Leon came out wearing a towel around his waist with a drum and a baton in his hands and never said anything to us. He just looked at us with a bad attitude, walked towards the front of the house and called a man who had a machete and a big club in his hands. "Watch them and make sure they don't go anywhere," he bellowed to the man.

We could not believe that Leon would do that to us. He had a very angry look on his face, and really behaved contrary to how we used to know him before. He then faced the high school area and started to beat the drum, shouting: "Ngoga's family is here, come and help me deal with them!" I couldn't believe what I was hearing coming from Leon's mouth! "Please Leon, please, if you don't want to hide us, please let us go!" we begged as he kept trying to alert the killers.

The killers didn't immediately respond and he got angry and shouted: "Why don't you all come quickly to help me kill these cockroaches?" I remember feeling numb where I was standing, and my mind flashed back to my experience in the sorghum field. I started to imagine seeing hordes of devilish looking killers swarming upon us and slicing us to pieces with their gruesome weapons . . . I was about to faint!

There was still no response from the killers 'den' probably due to the early hour, and after what seemed like an eternity, Leon went back into the house, leaving us guarded by the man at the gate. We didn't know what was going to happen next and were still in shock that friends as close to us as Leon and Lucille could do this to us.

We stood there pondering about our hopeless situation, when the man guarding us with the machete surprised us and whispered to us: "Come on all of you guys . . . pass through this hole in the fence and leave right now and go far away from here!" Without wasting a second, we quickly went through the hole and headed back to the bushes, thanking God for sparing us from death once again.

As we stumbled through the bushes Mom was looking at us with hurt etched all over her face. I could feel her deep anguish over the horrific things we were going through. It was now almost impossible for us to find people who we could trust, and were surviving by God's grace for the moment. Our journey was still ongoing and we didn't know whether we would see other days. That day we prayed in our hearts and thanked God for his mercy as we continued on our eventful journey.

It was now close to 6 o'clock in the morning, the time when many of the killers would begin their search for Tutsis. We were in the bushes trying our best to hide but were all terribly hungry. We had not eaten for almost two days and Bon-Fils was crying for something to eat. I myself was so hungry that I remember breaking a sorghum tree and trying to chew its stalk out of desperation. I was feeling badly in my stomach and was desperate to have something in there. Mom looked at me without saying anything. Oblivious to what I was doing, I looked back at her and saw tears streaming down her face. Those tears and the despairing look on her face saddened me immensely and jolted back my consciousness of the extraordinary pains she was enduring as a mother. My mind flashed back to the times when she was able to feed all of us properly before those terrible things started to happen, and the nagging questions as to why we had to suffer like this, flooded my brain again.

We dodged around in the bushes for some time, not knowing what to do, and later that day we ended up near the home of the parents of Mr. Laurent, my teacher from Junior High School. Mom thought we should try there to see if they would have pity on us. Truthfully, we were very apprehensive to do this as it was still daylight and we didn't know who to trust anymore. We had seen and experienced enough to know that people had drastically changed overnight. Nevertheless, we had to try something.

When we got there, we knocked on the door which was opened by Laurent's mother Bertha and his sister Mary. "Oh, thank God you're alive! Come in fast!" Bertha said, apparently surprised but relieved to see us. In my heart I thought to myself: "Maybe these people are going to be good to us and would not be like the others we met earlier!"

"You look very shaken and cold, please sit down and relax," said Mary, as she and Bertha enquired as to where we had been and how we were able to get to their house. They brought us some food and drink which we needed so badly, and after eating, Mom related to them what had happened to us so far. They were very compassionate and showed empathy towards us and we felt great for the moment.

My teacher Laurent, who lived next door to them, came in later and saw us there. He did not say much to us and went to his home shortly after. His behavior and attitude towards us was very troubling as it reminded us of how some of our previously close friends and neighbors had shown us an evil side lately. I prayed in my heart that he would not betray us. Bertha and Mary put us at ease and allowed us to stay overnight which we welcomed.

The next day we were still being treated well and sometime around midday they left us in the house and went next door to visit Laurent. By evening that day, Bertha and Mary came to us smiling, but I could detect a slight change in their body language. "We are sorry that we cannot keep you longer, as we are afraid that the killers will find you and destroy our home and take our stuff," Bertha said to my mother. Mom did not respond, and sat there dejectedly. "You will have to find another place to go," added Bertha. Mom sighed deeply, and I shuddered as I thought about the struggles we had to face again in the bushes with my little sister and kid brothers. I felt certain that my teacher had a key role in that decision. Lo and behold, while we were there waiting to leave by nightfall, he showed up and never said a word, but hung around without any show of emotion until we left the house.

We entered the dark bushes through their backyard and I knew we were in familiar territory once more when I started to hear the 'orchestra' of crickets and frogs and other types of nocturnal bush sounds whose rhythm continued incessantly, as if welcoming us to join their 'party.'

After walking for a while the rain started to fall. We struggled through the dark, falling down many times due to the slippery mud. It continued to rain very hard and after several hours we came upon another home whose occupants were mom's casual friends, and whose kids were her students at school. At that point she felt that since we couldn't tell who were good from bad anymore we just had to try and hope for the best.

When we got there she knocked on the door and Jezibel, the woman of the house, asked who it was. "It's me Marie-Jeanne," Mom replied. "Go away, I can't allow Tutsis in my house!" she retorted. "Please, let the kids come out of the rain and when it stops we will leave!" Mom pleaded. Jezibel kept insisting that we go away, until one of her kids said to her: "Please Mama, can you let our teacher come in from the rain with her kids?" and added: "We love our teacher Mommy, we don't want her to get hurt outside with her kids, would you please let her come in?"

Jezibel's kids pleaded with her several times until she gave in and opened the door for us. After letting us in, she said to us: "It's only because I love my kids so much I gave in to them—I wouldn't do this normally because I have hated you Tutsis so much my whole life. Thanks to my kids, they saved you tonight!" My mom then humbly said to her: "Thank you for allowing us to come in, Jezibel."

It was hard to understand Jezibel's brazenness in saying those things to our faces. When her kids saw us they felt compassionate and came closer to us and told their mother that we needed to get some warmth and something to eat. She brought us food and arranged a place for us to sleep in one room of her house. "All the stuff you see packed in these rooms were taken from the homes of fleeing Tutsis," Jezibel boasted as she walked us through the house.

We considered ourselves lucky that night to have been given a little break and not chased again from the house. Before we went to lie down, Jezibel said to us: "My husband Gregoire is coming back early in the morning so I want you to be up before he comes; I will wake you up so that you can go to hide because he'll definitely kill you if he sees you—I have no doubt about that!" That was one of the complexities of the situation—to see someone who we thought was a friend but hated Tutsis so much, being pressured by her children to protect us, at least briefly, from her husband who himself was a killer!

Since we had arrived there late after midnight, we didn't get much sleep but were thankful for the short rest. Jezibel woke us up early as planned and pleasantly surprised us when she said: "I'm going to hide you in my mother-in-law's house which has been abandoned since she passed away years ago."

We eagerly got out of the house and she took us to her mother-in-law's house which was not far away from hers. It was very small with a lot of holes in the ceiling. It also appeared to be badly maintained and looked like it was ready to fall down, but we didn't mind. She opened it and we went in quickly and she re-locked it from outside.

Some hours later we heard people talking outside her house about how many Tutsis they had killed at the roadblocks the night before. We peeped through some holes and saw that it was a group of men including Jezibel's husband Gregoire. They were celebrating the 'good work' they had done at the roadblocks and Gregoire told her to bring food and beer for them outside where they were sitting. We were not far from where they had gathered and became very scared listening to them, praying that they would not find us there.

To our dismay, about an hour later one of the guys started saying that he wanted to go to the little house we were in to put the stuff he had, and asked Jezibel if she could open the door for him. Gregoire told her to allow him to put his stuff there as they were like buddies. She tried to distract them by saying that she had lost the key, and Gregoire replied that it was okay they would break the lock and would find another lock later.

We started freaking out when we heard him say that, but Jezibel kept insisting that they do not put the stuff there. "I am going to break that house and see what's in there that Jezibel doesn't want us to see," shouted Gregoire to his friends. "Marie Jeanne and her kids are there, that's why!" Jezibel blurted out in a panic. "What? How could you hide Tutsis and you know that we don't want them!" Gregoire angrily retorted.

We were hearing everything and I became numb and scared and didn't know what to think or do except pray and wait. They continued arguing loudly with her and one guy then said: "Let's break down the door right now and cut those cockroaches into pieces." Jezibel and her children started begging them to let us go, but they refused and said: "We're going to set that house on fire and they'll die inside!" To our utter relief, Jezibel uncharacteristically continued to speak in our defense. "Please don't do it—I'll bring the key, but you should let them go somewhere else," she begged.

After a few minutes we heard the door opening, and we clung tightly to each other in a corner, shaking and praying to God to protect us there. I felt like a million needles were piercing through my body at the same time. Bon-Fils held on tightly to Mom while the rest of us held on to each other, praying. The only prayer I could manage to say was: "O lord, if this is the end, please take us to your good place to join our people!" After opening the door, one of those guys who we knew as Bienvenue came storming in with a machete . . .

★   ★   ★

REFLECTIONS ON CHAPTER 8

I am pained whenever I recall how some of the people who were close friends of my family and had benefited from their kindness over the years had turned their backs on us and treated us as scum when we sought refuge at their homes. I believe that they were simply misguided or selfish and never had love in their hearts to begin with, but had managed to mask their true feelings about us as a people.

The saddest part of all this was to see them reveal their enmity towards us, which overflowed at a time when we needed their friendship most. I truly hope that they have gone past their misconceptions about true friendship, and have been able to clear their consciences and forgive themselves for their acute betrayal at a time when their loyalty as friends truly mattered.

It was amazing to see that the kids of some of our so-called "friends" were more rational in their thinking and showed compassion for us when their parents did not. That's why kids are considered angels, and if only our hearts could become as pure as theirs, there would be far less hatred in our world.

CHAPTER 9

PILLAR OF STRENGTH

"I'm going to kill you now and cut you into pieces, you cockroaches!" Bienvenue shrieked as he entered the house. "Bienvenue, spare us please . . . . please let us go!" we screamed as he kept coming towards us with the machete upraised. "Please let us go, Bienvenue . . . please, please . . . . I beg you!" Mom continued screaming as she stood up with us trembling in fear behind her. "Jeanne, you are a Tutsi cockroach; . . . I don't care that you were my neighbor and have known you so many years; . . . you and your little cockroach kids have to die! I don't tolerate any Tutsi I see around me at all!" he angrily replied. Bienvenue then placed the machete to Mom's neck, violently shaking her at the same time. With tears streaming down my face, I was shaking uncontrollably with fear and Jeanette and my three little brothers held on tightly to me and Mom, with all of us screaming at the top of our lungs, pleading with him to let us live.

We continued begging and screaming while he continued to shake Mom violently, and after pleading with him for what seemed like an eternity, he slowly lowered the machete to his side as he finally appeared to regain some semblance of sanity. I believe God truly wanted us to remain alive for a reason, as Bienvenue had looked like he was not himself and was ready to kill us. After he calmed down and let go of Mom he said to us: "You need to leave this area and go somewhere else—I don't want to see you all around again! Even though I let you go this time, no one else would let you go if they catch you!"

Jezibel came into the room as Bienvenue turned to leave and after he and the group left Jezibel said to us: "I'm surprised that Bienvenue let you go because they don't spare any Tutsi they find—you are lucky people! You must leave as soon as possible before they show up again; if they do they might change their mind and kill you right away!" Hearing Jezibel talk that way caused me and my siblings to shiver in fear once more and we found it difficult to settle down after that experience.

We had to move on though, and it seemed like the only option left to us was to face whatever came our way, minute by minute, hour by hour, day by day! Jezibel gave us something to eat before we left and said to us that she can't guarantee that we will survive again. After that latest harrowing experience, I had reached the stage where my heart was ready to accept whatever happens to us. I prayed to God in my heart, saying: "Lord if anything happens to us, please take us to your place to meet our dad and loved ones who have gone!" Despite all that we were going through, we never lost strength to pray to God. Mom kept encouraging us in every step that we moved. She was the pillar of our strength!

As we entered the bushes once more, Mom had to again think about where we can go to find refuge, having experienced firsthand in the past weeks how so many people whom we thought were good friends had turned their backs on us. She looked at us sadly and told us we had no other choice but to try begging Bosco to keep us in his little shack again.

We stumbled through the bushes, hiding as usual and arrived at Bosco's shack just as darkness fell and walked straight in. "Please go back, I don't want you here, I don't want to see you here!" he shouted in panic as soon as he saw us. "Please Bosco, please help us" we begged. "We have nobody else to turn to. You are the only person we feel safe with, so can you help us, please?" Mom pleaded. It was very difficult to get him to accept as it was clear that he was genuinely scared, but after much persuasion he finally accepted and we went straight into our familiar 'hotel room.' Bosco was a very poor person who hardly had things to eat himself but he managed to get a little food for Bon-Fils to eat that night. Poor Bon-Fils gobbled up those welcome scraps of food so quickly as he was really hungry.

The next morning we got up and were sitting very still in that room trying to avoid making the slightest sound. After a while we suddenly heard what sounded like a large crowd of killers making their usual commotion. Bosco was sitting in the sun on a rock outside with the door closed and the Interahamwe group were running and chanting extermination songs. They came close to where Bosco was sitting and we heard them say: "Musazi, we want to check inside to see if any Tutsi snakes are in there!" On hearing this, we started trembling once again. My throat suddenly felt dry, and those millions of pins and needles started pricking me all over my body once more. "Oh no, not again; this could be the end this time!" I said to myself as I clutched on to Mom.

The killers kept bullying Bosco to open for them to search, but he tried to show his solidarity with them. "You know I hate Tutsis and can never allow them in my home!" he nonchalantly told them. "Open the door now, we want to see for ourselves!" they insisted. Bosco got scared and lost his bravado and quickly opened the door. The leader of the group rushed inside, telling the others to stay outside as the place was small. He passed through the open area where Bosco cooks and sleeps and came straight to that dark room where we were sitting very scared, clutching each other tightly.

"It's Marie-Jeanne, the teacher and her kids who are here in this house!" Fidele shouted to his followers as he saw us. For some strange reason he didn't threaten us or say a word to us, and instead returned outside amidst shouts from many in his group who were screaming "they must be killed, what are we waiting for?" We seized that brief moment and all of us started praying incessantly.

Fidele, who was known to us, suggested to the group that we be spared that day if we could give them some of our belongings. By God's grace they agreed and he came back inside and found us still holding on to each other and praying. He looked at us for a moment and said to Mom: "Your mother has been good to me and helped me in many ways, so I won't let these people kill you and your kids! They are ready to kill you, but I'll just give you this option that could save you today, as they won't leave without getting something!"

In my young brain I couldn't understand what he was getting at, but he continued: "The option for you is to try to find what materials or money you own to give these people so that they can let you and your kids go—If not, they will kill you for sure."

"I . . . I don't have any money, it is all gone, but I can try to go to a neighbor who is keeping the stuff from our house; th . . . that's the only thing I may be able to try at this time," was Mom's stammering reply.

Fidele agreed but told Mom that she should only take the baby and leave the rest of us there. Mom insisted that we also go with her but he refused. Fidele went back outside and told the group about the plan, and Mom compulsively hugged us with sadness and in tears and said "Don't worry, my children, God will protect you until I return. Keep on praying for all of us."

Mom's emotional hug and the sadness we saw in her eyes flooded us with apprehension about her safe return. We became fearful that we may never see her and Bon-Fils again, and instinctively screamed out in agony "Please don't hurt our mother, we need her back with us," as she left with that bunch of killers following closely behind her. It was painful to see her go, and as they faded off into the distance all we could do was try to console each other, still sobbing and praying that she and Bon-Fils would come back to us soon.

Mom was escorted to our neighbor Jackson's house by the group. She later told us that when they got there, she was shocked by Jackson's attitude towards her. He was very aggressive and told her she should not come close to where he was standing. She, nonetheless, approached where he was and told him: "You see, I'm in a big problem here. These people will only let me go if I give them some of the stuff from my house. Would you please give me some of my things to give to them so that they can let me go back to my kids, please?" He looked at her from head to toe as if she had said something inappropriate and laughed out loudly in a sarcastic way, mocking her.

"Jeanne, I can't allow anything belonging to Tutsi to come out of this house! If I do I won't be able to find anywhere to socialize with other Hutus anymore! I will be excluded in the society for good and will no longer be called a good Hutu!" was his bold response.

Mom could not believe Jackson's words and attitude towards her, as he was always respectful and kind to her in the past. "Would you at least give them a radio and maybe that would help?" she insisted, knowing that she was running out of options. Jackson refused to budge and continued to mock and hurl insults at her. Mom threw up her hands in despair, saddened to see that even a person like Jackson who she treated as a son had allowed the evil perpetrated by others to work within him and change him so radically 'overnight.'

Fidele appeared to have been truly protective of Mom that day and started to chide Jackson. "Come on, man, give us at least one item and save this woman's life today! She was your neighbor, and she is a good person. That is why I just want them to let her go!" he scolded.

"Do whatever you want to her I don't care! Nothing belonging to her can come out of this house for the sake of protecting her! Tutsis do not have the right to live among us!" Jackson heartlessly replied. Looking sternly at Jackson, Fidele said to him: "You will be responsible for whatever happens to her because you have the option to stop it for now!"

The killers were still there getting impatient and waiting for the next move, as Jackson still did not respond. Mom felt there was nothing more she could say or ask of Jackson who appeared to have completely changed into another person. "Thank you Jackson for what you did to me! Don't worry; God will be with me throughout!" she told him dejectedly. Fidele and his group then started to walk away, with Mom and Bon-Fils following behind. They were now squarely in the hands of the killers with no other way of helping themselves.

As they walked away, the group kept arguing whether they should kill Mom or let her go. They took her on the main road across from our burnt out home, exposing her for everyone in the area to see. Many of the killers were eager to kill her but somehow it didn't happen and instead they kept talking and arguing about what they should do. That scenario was really unusual in the atmosphere that existed at the time. Mom felt that God wanted to keep her alive for the time being, and kept praying in her heart.

The novelty of this unusual scene may have also confused the killers. Some of them who she knew very well started saying that they didn't feel like killing her and didn't have the energy to do it. Others were saying "we have her in our hands so we can kill her whenever we want!" They paraded her through the streets with Bon-Fils still on her back, mocking her throughout the day. She had become the talk of the town and people were very surprised that they had not yet killed her.

Strangely, the group met with the local authorities to discuss her fate and they decided that she being a woman they would kill her at their own leisure. I guess God wanted us to see each other again before our end came. The killers took her to the nearby home of a disabled old man named Gatwaza close to one of their meeting points. When the old man saw her he was stunned to see that she was still alive and was curious to know why the killers had brought her there. They did not explain much to him but told him that he must keep her and not allow her to go anywhere. At that time his sixteen year old granddaughter was living with him. She was happy to see my mother alive but at the same time was worried about what was going to happen. Gatwaza and his granddaughter gave Mom and Bon-Fils a place to rest their tired bodies after having been dragged all over the village that day.

By evening when Mom did not return to us, Bosco got scared and thought she might have been killed. Jeanette, my two brothers, and I were there huddled together in a corner praying and comforting each other when he came into the room and said: "You have to go and look for your mother to see whether she is still alive or not! I don't want you to stay here anymore, not even for a few minutes!" Being the kids that we were, and feeling that it wouldn't make a difference, we did not insist much for him to keep us, but before we left I encouraged my brothers by telling them: "Don't worry guys, let's just keep praying in our hearts so that we'll find Mom soon!"

It was still bright outside with people still walking on the roads and killers still searching for victims. We knew that we could be killed if we stayed in the open places so we went through the bushes, trying to hide. While walking through the bushes going down Rupango hill we heard voices of people we knew very well saying: "Where are those little cockroaches? Where have they disappeared to already?" We all got scared and our hearts jumped but we had to find ways to hide. It was very frightening as we felt certain that they were looking for us, so we sat still as rocks in the bushes without letting out a breath.

We sat quietly in the middle of those trees, and while sitting there we could see them passing by not very far from us. "Wherever you are, come out you little cockroaches!" they shouted, cutting bushes as they passed. We kept still and could still see them as they went over to the other side of the hill. After a while we heard them saying: "We can't find them, they were probably killed by others! Let's move on!"

Relieved but still frozen with fear, we looked at each other's faces without moving, waiting until we knew for sure they had left before we move on. When we felt satisfied that they were gone, we all took a deep breath and thanked God for protecting us. While still standing there and reflecting on our miraculous escape, Pascal looked at us with such strong courage and said: "Guys, be strong and don't worry about anything! Let's just keep moving and try to find Mom and Bon Fils. Our journey is not over yet!"

It was a struggle for us to determine where to go, as roadblocks and killers were everywhere. We thought our best option was to try to go to Jackson's house where we knew Mom was taken earlier that day. There was one problem with that option though—It was getting dark and we did not know the way through the bushes, and using the main road would be suicidal. We decided instead to keep moving through the bushes and try to figure out which home we can go to and ask for refuge and to find out if anything was known about our mother.

After walking for a while we landed smack in the middle of a banana plantation and saw Godfrey who had done some construction work on our house in the past. It was already getting dark so we never expected to see anyone around there at that time, but luckily we saw him before he saw us. He was cutting a bunch of green bananas from the field. We couldn't tell how he would respond but took a chance and approached him. "Hey, you guys are still alive?" was his immediate reaction upon seeing us. "I thought you may have been killed because the killers were looking for you everywhere!" he added.

We replied that we had seen them looking for us but they didn't find us. "You're lucky kids; as soon they knew you were alive they came to look for you wanting to kill you!"

"We are glad to see you Godfrey; at least you are going to help us!" I said to him, and without waiting for a response, asked: "Have you heard anything about our mother?" to which he replied: "All day long the killers argued whether to kill your mother or not, but never did so. They took her to your neighbor Gatwaza to watch her until they decide when to kill her. I don't recommend you go there because you all will be killed together."

"So then would you please help us and hide us?" I promptly asked him. He turned around and I could see that his body language had immediately changed, and he said to me: "Find somewhere else to hide but I cannot help you!" He then started ignoring us and went back to cutting his bananas.

We were very disappointed that Godfrey had refused to help us but at least we knew what was going on with Mom. We asked him if he could tell us how to get to Gatwaza's house without passing through the streets and he gave us some directions through the bushes. We left with a lot of worry in our hearts and it was already dark so we couldn't figure out well the directions he had given us. We kept moving through the night but couldn't find the right path to follow due to the darkness and actually ended up right where we started, at the top of Rupango hill near the veterinary shed. When we got near to the shed, we froze as we heard people talking, not knowing whether they were killers or not. As soon as I heard them, I told Jeanette and my brothers that we should avoid going towards their location.

We kept walking and saw a house on the other side of Rupango hill. I looked at that quaint little house and had a gut feeling that if we go there it could be a little better for us that night. I don't know what made me feel that way, but I felt confident about trying it. "Guys, you see that house across there, let's go there!" I said to my siblings. "No, no Macwa, we can't go there!" they immediately responded in unison.

Trusting others to have pity on us had become very difficult for them. For me, I just wanted us to keep trying to see whether there would be someone who would have pity on us. I told them we should try because I felt within my heart that it could be safer for us to go there that night.

We headed towards the house and as we walked I told them that we should keep praying and ask God to continue to be on our side. We arrived at that house and knocked on the door which someone opened for us. As soon as the occupants saw us they looked upon us with pity and embraced us and took us quickly into the house. They seemed very poor financially but rich in compassion. We felt that they knew who we were when they said to us: "Thank God you're alive! You were being searched for everywhere throughout the afternoon and evening, and the whole community knew that you were still alive because of your mother!"

We were very cold after being outside for so long and the clothes we were wearing were badly torn and our bodies were pretty much exposed. They lit some firewood and sat us around the fire in a circle to get some warmth and then went to find some food for us. They talked to us very compassionately and tried to comfort us as much as they could. It was the best we had been treated in weeks and we felt like humans once more. It was refreshing to me to actually come across some Hutus in our area who were still thinking and acting with pity towards unfortunate Tutsis.

I was thankful to God for leading us there to at least allow us some temporary solace and rest for our frail bodies without fear. They started telling us what they had heard throughout the day about our mother's ordeal and also confirmed what Godfrey had told us about where she had been taken with my brother. Those people showed us love that night, and appeared unhappy about what was going on and were praying for the horrible massacres to stop. They also prayed for us and read us some bible verses. I will always be grateful to them for demonstrating to us that night that some of their people were still humane. I can also never forget their simplicity and goodness of heart despite their poverty, and pray that God will reward them for their goodness to us.

When morning came they left us in the house and went to Gatwaza's house to tell Mom that we are still alive. As soon as they returned they told us that they had spoken with her, and we immediately insisted that we must go there to join her before the killers get on the streets. They were of course afraid of what may happen to us but we needed to find Mom and then figure out our fate after. When we arrived there Mom was in tears but so happy to see us. We cried with joy for once, hugged her and thanked God that we were able to see each other again.

Gatwaza and his granddaughter offered us some water which we used to wash ourselves, the first opportunity we actually had to do so since we went into hiding in early April, and it was then early May. Our bodies were covered with mud and our clothes were filled with lice which made our skin itchy all the time. They cooked beans and sweet potatoes for us which we ate and then laid down to have some long needed sleep.

We spent the whole day there, thankful for being reunited with Mom and having the knowledge that whatever happens to us, at least we will all be together. Gatwaza was very afraid that the killers might change their minds at any time and come to kill us all there. He could do nothing else but wait on them, as we were being watched. We had become 'battle-weary' due to all of the pain and hardship we had endured throughout the month of April and which was still continuing into the month of May, so we prayed continuously and asked God to be with us all the way.

★　★　★

REFLECTIONS ON CHAPTER 9

The multiplicity of dramatic incidents we encountered within a very short period of time as described in this chapter, is a continuation of the extreme horrors we faced in the previous one. The worst part of this series of experiences was our unprecedented betrayal by close friends and people we considered as 'family.' I will never understand how someone as close to us as Jackson had so adamantly refused to hand over our own belongings to would-be killers, despite being begged to do so by their leader as a condition for sparing my mother's life. In contrast, the lead killer of the group showed compassion for her and went out of his way to prevent her from being killed.

The fact that my mom is still alive today despite her multiple 'appointments with death,' is testimony of God's power over our own.

CHAPTER 10

FAREWELL TO ANGELIC BROTHERS

"Marie-Jeanne's boys must be killed today as ordered by the Mayor! She and her daughter must stay with you until we decide whether to kill them or make them our slaves and we will be coming for the boys later today!" Those were the chilling messages delivered by a bunch of ruthless Interahamwe killers to Gatwaza as he sat on the street outside his home. Gatwaza's jaw fell open as he tried to process the messages. The Interahamwe killers were gone as quickly as they came, screaming and chanting as they paraded through the streets with their banana leaf costumes and bloodstained weapons.

It was May 9th 1994, a date I will never forget. "What will I do? . . . What will I do? . . . I don't know what to do!" said Gatwaza, as he hustled into the house dragging on his crutches. "Marie-Jeanne, Marie-Jeanne, I have terrible news!" he said dejectedly to Mom. "They will be coming for your boys later today to kill them, but you and your daughter will be okay!" he continued. I felt like I was hit by a bus and couldn't feel my feet, and as I looked at Mom she was holding her chest with a river of tears streaming down her cheeks.

Mom was very distraught and took us all together in the room and told us that we need to pray and let God be in our hearts. "My children . . . pray and feel God within you . . . No matter what is going to happen, just know that God will take care of us," she moaned, as we all went down on our knees in tears, praying passionately.

After we stopped praying, Philbert and Pascal stood up and seemed ready for whatever destiny was to befall them. I remember trying to console myself and thinking without any anger that those people were blind to what they were doing to us and they would suffer more than us in the end. My young brothers were not afraid as they looked at peace within themselves and in my mind were braver than all those cowardly killers put together. I will never forget the tranquil aura they exhibited in preparation for what they knew was coming. Looking at their faces and the calm acceptance that they exuded gave me an innate strength which I had not felt before. We all gathered around and sat together on the same chair, and held each other's hands.

Our youngest brother Bon-Fils was too young to know anything but I am sure he felt that abnormal things were happening, having already seen what we had been through so far. He was holding on tightly to Mom who cuddled him closely against her chest with a dejected look on her face.

A few minutes later the killers came into the room, including Sanani, one we knew very well. My grandfather had been a very close friend of his father and had given him a plot of land many years before to build the home in which Sanani and his siblings grew up. Their friendship was so close that Sanani's younger sister Christine had served as a bridesmaid at my mother's wedding in 1977. Shockingly, Sanani had come with other killers to take my brothers to kill them.

"Sanani! Sanani! How could you of all people do this to us? Is this what you choose to do in return for the kindness we showed to your family over the years? May God forgive you Sanani!" Mom wailed, shaking her head in disbelief.

The scene was very traumatic for all of us as we realized that they were dead serious about murdering our angelic little brothers. It was too much to bear and we all became hysterical. We begged the killers to take all of us without leaving anyone behind, as we were unable to accept the thought of them suffering such agony alone. The group leader's cold hearted response to our pleadings was "Shut up! You will have your own time; we have to take the boys right now!"

Bon-Fils was in my mother's arms and he held on to her tightly as he saw those men who looked like monsters in those weird costumes armed to the teeth, with cruel looks in their eyes.

"No, no! Not my kids! Take all of us, don't leave us behind!" Mom screamed at them. Philbert and Pascal were not even crying or shouting and bravely walked towards Bon-Fils and each held one of his hands and said: "We are going to join Daddy in Heaven Bon-Fils!"

They flanked Bon-Fils on either side as they held his hands, and the three of them slowly walked towards the killers. Mom screamed loudly again, with me and Jeanette doing the same, begging the killers to take us all.

The group ignored our pleas and took our three precious brothers and walked them to our burnt-out house about five minutes away, where they slaughtered their little bodies and threw them into our large septic tank in the yard. That moment was very devastating for us—we needed to die too that day! Their killings were witnessed by many people, none of whom lifted a finger to stop the brutal slaughter of those defenseless infants, but many of them formed a procession following the killers as they happily celebrated their evil deed.

"Hutu Power! Hutu Power! We have exterminated some little cockroaches and saved our people the trouble of having them grow up to cause problems!" chanted the killers as they hustled along the road.

As we sat in sorrow in Gatwaza's house we could hear a lot of chatter as people gathered in the street. We learned from their gossip that Pascal tried begging them to spare their lives, but as he started to speak he was viciously attacked with a machete, and succumbed instantly. Philbert and Bon-Fils suffered a similar fate soon after. It was deeply hurtful to us and we were all crying out in mental anguish. We were no longer afraid of dying because we wanted to follow our precious little Angels of God who had just been taken away from us. I was ready to die then because the world no longer meant anything to me!

Around four o'clock that evening a leading Interahamwe killer, Boniface, who had many Tutsi victims 'under his belt,' stormed into Gatwaza's house with a gun in his hand saying he had orders from the Mayor's office to kill us. He appeared evil and spoke crudely to us as he led us outside and lined us up for everyone around to see. He started humiliating us with anti-Tutsi sentiments and said to us: "I'm going to shoot you so that you can die quickly; that would be the best thing I can do for you!"

Mom, Jeanette and I all appeared to have lost the will to resist or beg for our lives and stood there looking at him in defiance. "Give this acid to your girls and drink some yourself," he barked, as he looked at Mom and reached out his hand with a bottle in it. "Why don't you give it to us yourself?" Mom replied, as she refused to take the bottle. Boniface kept looking at us scornfully and we continued to look him in the eye with defiance.

"I have killed so many cockroaches but I don't want to touch your blood in my hands! You don't have a life and it's just a matter of time for you anyway!" he said to Mom with lesser aggression. To our surprise, he left suddenly without harming us, with the other killers quickly following after him. Mom, Jeanette and I quickly walked back into Gatwaza's house to get away from the curious crowd which had gathered to look.

Later that same day news spread in the neighborhood that Boniface had fallen off the back of a pickup truck in Gitikinini Center and struck his head, and had died on the spot. On hearing the news I could not help but feel that he was simply being punished for what he had done, and I said to Mom: "Well, he has shed the blood of so many innocent people, but he never thought that he can die too someday!" Mom looked at me without saying anything but I could not withhold my thoughts.

"I wish he would have gotten a chance to realize that what he did to others was against the word of God, and that we are all children of God who deserve to live until **He** is ready to take us!" I concluded.

That day, we were very devastated by the loss of our brothers and our own close shave with death. None of us slept that night, and I had many haunting images in my mind about the intense fear which my little brothers must have experienced during those painfully long five minutes leading up to their deaths. Mom was more devastated than we were, and one could tell by her facial expression and body language that her heart was inflamed.

The next day the three of us sat outside Gatwaza's house, visible to people passing in the street but we no longer cared about our safety.

A few people came to us, talking and expressing their sorrow, but the majority passed by and looked at us with scorn and contempt. It was unbelievably crazy to see how previously good thinking people had been watching and relishing our torture, and their attitude and what they were saying gave the impression that we were no longer human beings.

The frequency at which the Interahamwe terrorized us in Gatwaza's house the previous day must have overwhelmed the old man. Poor Gatwaza had not slept since the initial episode with my brothers and was continuously strutting around on his crutches muttering to himself for most of the day. Several people stopped and talked to him in the street, and whatever they said to him seemed to calm him down after a while, but what he told us later made us realize that they had actually scared him.

"Jeanne, you escaped being killed many times, but I'm scared that other killers may come around here and kill you!" he said to Mom in a frightened tone as he walked into the house. "I don't want them to come and take my cows and the few things I have after they kill you!" he added.

We remained indifferent as he told us we must leave, and started walking fearlessly onto the street without a thought about where we were heading. As we walked past the home of a community leader, Nkunzabo, he saw us and said: "Don't keep walking on the street like that in the middle of the day; come into my house!" His wife Dorothy took us into the house and offered us a place to sit and relax and when evening came she offered us some food and a place to lie down and rest.

The next day we saw Nkunzabo leaving the house, and upon his return several hours later he was accompanied by Interahamwe killers from the area. He acted as if they had followed him but by the way they were interacting, we suspected that he was in cahoots with them. Dorothy was somehow willing to help us, but her husband seemed to have taken us in simply to be killed. We survived that day as the killers left without threatening or harming us, but the next day Nkunzabo left the house again and when he returned that evening he was with a killer named Shinani.

Shinani's family were close neighbors and friends to my father's family and they had shared good mutual relationships over the years. From what I had seen myself as a child growing up, Shinani and other members of his family visited our house to socialize from time to time, and we also occasionally visited their house which was situated across the street from where we lived.

That evening, it was difficult to recognize Shinani as the person we had known before. He had a demonic look in his eyes and held up a menacing sword in his hand as he walked in. He looked in the direction where we were sitting and started yelling loudly and threatening us. "I'm taking this girl to show me where you put all the guns and other things you got from RPF!" he yelled out to Mom as he hustled towards me. I started shaking and felt like I was about to pass out. "You can't take my daughter! If you want to kill us, kill us all here!" Mom yelled at the top of her voice, while Nkunzabo just looked on with a half smile on his face.

Shinani started pulling me from where I was sitting as Mom held on to me with both hands. "Leave her alone or take us all and kill us if that's what you want!" Mom and Jeanette shouted, as he pushed them against the wall. I myself was terrified, and screamed: "Leave me alone or kill me right here!"

Shinani ignored our pleadings and pulled me out of the house. Mom and Jeanette tried to follow but he pushed them to the ground and dragged me into the street.

Darkness was starting to creep in as he dragged me along the main road. I kept crying out loudly telling him to let me go or kill me, but he kept on dragging me, oblivious to my screams and to the cuts and bruises I had already sustained on my knees and legs. Still screaming all the way, Shinani dragged me towards his family's home, while onlookers on the street took in the scene without intervening. "Don't you dare do anything to that girl!" his brother shouted as he dragged me inside the doorway. "She is a family neighbor! Please, let that child go, please let her go!" he pleaded. They argued for a while as I sat cringed on the floor, still begging, frightened, and desperately wanting to leave.

Shinani eventually relented and pushed me back outside, dragged me into some bushes near to our burnt-out home and started stripping off my clothes. I tried to resist and kept on crying and begging him to let me go, but he put the sword to my neck and kept insulting me saying that we are snakes and cockroaches. Every time I raised my arms to try to stop what he was doing, he beat me with the sword all over my body, and my hands and other parts of my body started to bleed. I continued to cry and scream but he tore all my clothes away and threw me on the ground with anger, held my two hands together and sexually assaulted me there.

Shinani left me in that bush bleeding and unable to walk properly due to the cuts and bruises I had sustained. I covered my private areas with whatever pieces of my clothing was left and dragged myself back to Nkunzabo's house to look for Mom and Jeanette. I didn't see anyone in the street, but I felt like I was no longer alive anyway and wished that somebody would come and kill me and end my life there and then.

When I arrived at Nkunzabo's house and Mom saw my condition she held me in her arms and cried so hard, almost losing her mind. I told her what had happened and she and Dorothy quickly took me into the house and washed me all over, gave me some clothes and put me to lie down on a bed. My body was hurting all over and I couldn't rest comfortably on the bed.

Mom cried the entire night, bemoaning what had happened to me. She had just lost her precious sons and now just four days later she was going through the pain of knowing that her daughter had been tortured and raped. I wanted to die and didn't care about survival anymore. I was still an innocent 14 year old girl, and I felt crushed in my spirit. There was such a deep sadness in me which caused me to question why I was still alive, as I felt I had truly lost the will to live. My heart was severely wounded after so much we had been through.

Around midday the following day we were inside the house with the door closed when killers came to the house again. "Open the door Jeanne!" yelled Sanani and others from outside. We didn't respond and he kept banging loudly on the door and said again: "Open the door Jeanne! If I am able to get in I will torture you so badly and then kill you!" to which Dorothy replied: "Don't you feel you have done enough to her? Why don't you go away?" Dorothy never opened the door and they left after threatening to return.

Our drama continued later that evening when Shinani and another killer came to the house, each armed with a machete. Upon seeing them, I became instantly terrified and held on tightly to Jeanette's hands. My terror turned into confusion when Shinani threatened to kill Mom and was accosted by his co-killer. "You know Jeanne is a good woman; if you kill her I will kill you also!" were the unusual words we heard coming from the lips of his co-killer.

"She has to die!" Shinani insisted, as he started beating Mom with the flat part of his machete. Nkunzabo came in while he was beating her, but never stopped him, and what he said next was simply unbelievable. "Why don't you kill her instead of torturing her?" he said matter-of-factly to Shinani who fortunately ignored him. The two killers kept arguing and then forcefully took Mom out of the house and headed towards our burnt-out home.

Mom did not return to Nkunzabo's house that night, causing much worry for Jeanette and I. The next morning Dorothy appeared unwilling to keep us any longer and told us that we must go and find Mom wherever she was. We didn't know where to go and prayed that Mom was still alive.

We walked aimlessly through the streets, ignoring the possibility of meeting killers on the way. We asked a few neighbors along the way whether they had heard anything about Mom and they all said no. Not getting any information and not knowing what to do, we returned to Nkunzabo's house. "You're not coming back here! Go and find your mother wherever she may be!" he yelled, as soon as he saw us.

We continued walking along the street mindless of our safety, while people were starting to come out of their homes, including Interahamwe about to go to 'work.' One elderly woman who knew us very well saw us and immediately called out to us saying: "Oh my Lord, you children will be killed if they see you!" She quickly led us from the open street area and through some lesser used paths away from the main road and told us that Mom was rescued the night before by someone she knew.

We followed the woman, quickly moving through some bushes, and she took us to the house of a man named Saidi where we found Mom. She hugged us with tears in her eyes and we were so happy to see her alive. Saidi showed empathy for our situation and told us that Mom and Dad were good to him in the past and he would help us as much as he can.

Saidi told us that he had a good neighbor named Jonathan who he would ask to help also. Jonathan later came to his house and we realized he was someone we had known. He talked with us for a while and then told Mom: "There is a big possibility that you all will be killed. I want to take your younger daughter who is around my kids' age group and keep her with them; at least all of you won't die at the same time!" Saidi then asked Mom if she would allow her to go, and she agreed.

Jeanette being the only sibling I had left, I started to cry, thinking that I might not see her again. She was also crying and Mom comforted her by telling her that with God's grace we would see each other again. We hugged for a while and she waved goodbye as she disappeared through the bushes with Jonathan.

"Some of my neighbors are not good people and would immediately inform the killers if they know you are here," Saidi told us as he looked for a secure hiding place for us. Later that day, he went to Gitikinini shopping center and heard that some killers were aware that he is hiding us in his home. He of course denied it, but as he got back home he immediately changed our hiding place.

That night, Mom related to me what had happened the evening before when Shinani took her away from Nkunzabo's house. "My child, they took me to the top of the septic tank at our old home, and Shinani started beating me with a machete. He insulted me and told me to throw myself into the tank on top of my kids, which I refused!" He continued beating me with the machete until some people from the crowd surprisingly asked him to let me go. He eventually stopped and told me to go back to Nkunzabo's house!"

God had somehow been there for Mom throughout, as the killers could not find the courage to kill her despite the many close encounters she had with them. As she walked back to Nkunzabo's house, she instinctively glanced around and observed that Shinani was still following her. Not trusting him, she darted into the bushes and he followed after her but could not find her. She kept running through the bushes and was able to reach Saidi's home in Nyarube not very far from Nkunzabo's home, and he accepted to hide her.

Saidi was one of the few people who were very concerned about what was happening and wanted to help rescue people even though he didn't have much to offer, but his heart was enough. He even went against some of his family's wishes, as they had continually warned him against keeping Tutsis in his house. Mom overheard him saying to some of them that she and Dad had helped him when he needed it, so he felt obligated to help us hide to save our lives. He also told them that they should not be unkind to Tutsis as we are human beings like they are!

After hearing that some of Saidi's family did not want us there, we became afraid once more and started to pray all over again for God to protect us. We had already lost a lot of people throughout the country, and many other Tutsi women had been tortured and sexually assaulted, and killed in some instances. The pain had become very heavy within our hearts and we had no idea how much more we would have to endure because the genocide was still going on in so many areas. The only thing we could do was to pray constantly and have God within our hearts.

★   ★   ★

REFLECTIONS ON CHAPTER 10

As a kid growing up I was taught by my parents to be conscious of my thoughts and ask for forgiveness to God if ever I thought badly about anyone. During certain periods of the genocide, especially the events I have just described in this chapter, those teachings were tearing me apart as it became too difficult to avoid thinking the worst about those evil people.

I tried to tell God that I love my enemies despite all the wrongs they were doing to us, but I knew deep down that those were just hollow words and was not what I felt in my heart! My heart was so deeply wounded by what had happened to me and my brothers and I couldn't get rid of those monsters from my mind. Over time, with God's help I was able to discard that burden I was carrying in my heart by placing their fate in His hands and asking Him to help me avoid having bad thoughts about them.

I sometimes love to remind myself about the best moments I had with each and every one of my family who were killed, especially my dad and my innocent baby brothers, and focus deeply on them as if they were present physically with me. I do that because I want to keep their good memories alive in my heart as my greatest treasures, as it helps me to be strong.

During their brief stay on earth, I was blessed to have them in my life, as they brightened my days and put smiles and laughter in our household. I am thankful that I experienced the friendliness and love they poured on me every single day that I spent with them. May the Lord bless their souls!

CHAPTER 11

SHELTERED BY MUSLIMS

"Saidi, I'm so worried about my little niece Chantal who I heard is still alive," Mom said to Saidi as he brought us food one day. "How do you know she is still alive?" Saidi replied. "A Tutsi neighbor who we met in the bush a few days ago told me that she was hiding near an Interahamwe headquarters and I am worried about her," Mom lamented. "Would it be asking too much for you to try to find out where she is and bring her to stay with us?"

Saidi was happy to give it a try and by the next day was able to locate Chantal and brought her to us. "Oh, Chantal, we are so happy that you are alive!" we all shouted as we embraced her. With tears streaming down her face, she replied: "I'm happy to see you all too! I thought all of you may have been killed!" Seeing our joy on being reunited, Saidi offered to ask his good friend Gerard if he could help to protect her. He later spoke with Gerard who was also a friend of Chantal's dad Vincent, and he readily agreed to hide her in his family's home.

That night, he took her to Gerard's home, with the understanding that she would stay there during the day and join us at night so we can find time to comfort each other. We did not ask her much about her ordeals since the genocide started nor did we tell her what we had been through. Knowing that we still had challenges ahead, we did not want to risk weakening each other.

We had not heard anything about my younger sister Jeanette since she had left to stay with Jonathan's family and hoped that she was safe. Mom and I prayed constantly but sometimes we could not help but break down and cry because of the deep hurt we were carrying. The rapid succession and extraordinary level of trauma we had faced over the past months was starting to take its' toll, especially on Mom. One day without warning she appeared to have lost her will. "Kids, I'm tired of hiding like an animal and facing so much abuse!" she said to Chantal and I as we sat quietly talking one evening. "Let's go and sit on the streets and let them kill us instead of continuing to live this way! It's just not fair to us!" she added in a serious tone.

Even though I was crushed in spirit and deeply hurt within myself, I was not ready to die then, and my inner voice kept telling me not to give up. I could feel Mom's pain, but I had to bring her back to her senses. I drew closer to her and held her hand lovingly and said: "Mom, please don't give up; let's keep on hiding and God will determine what he wants for us." She listened and pondered for a while and then held on to me tightly and started to cry and said: "My child, don't worry, I won't give myself to them; if they find us and it's our time to die we will have no choice! Thanks for your inspiring words, ma Cherie!"

About five days into our stay with Saidi, he received a 'tip-off' from one of his Muslim friends who told him that some killers were overheard planning to search his house that night. The Interahamwe suspected that he was hiding Tutsis and threatened to kill Saidi and any 'cockroaches' they find in his house. Saidi was very perturbed by the news, but insisted that he was not going to give up on us no matter what.

Saidi was one of the few persons we had come across who was truly good at heart, in contrast to most of the people who had become so monstrous. As a young girl, what I had seen and experienced in those few months was beyond imagining and my heart and mind were saturated with pain. I was deeply hurt and couldn't fathom how so many people had turned inhuman so rapidly, and was scared about what the killers would do to me next if they found me. And yes, they were ready again to come and search for us to kill us that night!

Meanwhile, Saidi was busy thinking about where he could move us to before the Interahamwe showed up. He finally decided to take us to one of his trusted Muslim friends named Ndekezi who had agreed to receive us that night as soon as darkness fell.

We hid in the bushes outside Saidi's house for most of the day, and just before nightfall Saidi met Mom and I there. "Saidi, I hope it's not too much to ask, but can we meet briefly to say goodbye to Chantal before we leave?" Mom asked as soon as he arrived. "No problem, Miss Jeanne, just follow me," he replied. He took us near to Jonathan's house and left us in the bushes and went in and brought her to see us. We hugged and cried together briefly, told her what was happening and prayed together for God's continued protection. We embraced again and said good bye and sauntered into the darkness of the woods.

We walked for quite some time and eventually reached Ndekezi's house safely without being seen. He was there to welcome us and immediately put us at ease. "Don't worry, I will do my best to keep you safe with Allah's help," he said to us with a broad smile. "I feel bad about what is happening in our country and all that has happened to you!" It was refreshing to see another person like Saidi who had the heart and courage to help us despite the risk to their lives also.

Ndekezi was single, and his older sister Laura lived with him. She also showed her willingness to help us relax and did what she could to help. Not long after we arrived she cooked for us and gave us water in buckets to wash ourselves at the back of the house. It was only our second opportunity to wash in about two months. Because of the lengthy period since I had my last wash, I looked at the bucket of water as though it was holy water from heaven! Mom came to help me wash myself because I really needed help to get that thick layer of dirt out from my body. After washing myself I felt much more human! Mom did the same and told me that she also felt better.

Laura cooked some cassava and stewed fish for us, and for the first time since the genocide started we were going to eat some decent food cooked with love! I felt like I was dreaming and did not want that dream to end!

"Let me show you where you can lie down and get some long overdue sleep," Laura said to us after eating. Feeling fairly safe for the first time in months, Mom and I tried our best to fall asleep, but just couldn't do so. We had gotten used to being scared and unsettled for too long! The next day, Ndekezi took us into one of the darker rooms in the house so we could hide there during the day.

Throughout that day we could hear groups of killers running around in the street not too far away chanting their death songs and bragging about their accomplishments. It had become common knowledge in Kibuye and other parts of the country that many Muslims were against what was happening and had refused to participate in the genocide so we were happy to be among them! "I have seen so many unbelievable things happen since this shameful genocide started," Ndekezi told us that evening. "Thousands of people who tried to hide in the churches were killed! Killers even came to our mosque looking for Tutsis to kill but our followers told them what they were doing was wrong and they will be cursed!" he added. Ndekezi was clearly saddened by what he had seen, and it was refreshing for us to have a conversation with someone who didn't change or become like so many of the others we had encountered.

The people of that small community were trying their best to help us Tutsis. Several households were giving refuge to a few people, and some of those not actually doing so were helping to feed those people. A large majority of people were engaged in hunting and killing Tutsis, so the country was virtually shut down and food was becoming scarce. The community had been searched multiple times but the killers rarely succeeded in finding anyone, as those good Samaritans maintained strict confidentiality and found all possible ways to properly conceal the people they were hiding.

That was about to change, however, for within a week of our arrival at Ndekezi's house we were hiding inside around midday one day when we heard a loud commotion outside and the sound of footsteps running into the house. "I saw the police and soldiers heading this way but hopefully they won't come here!" Ndekezi shouted as he came to us out of breath. "Stay where you are and don't be afraid; I'm going to sit outside and see what happens!"

We sat trembling in fear in the room as Ndekezi ran back outside, as he looked very afraid. Mom and I held on to each other in the room and started to pray that those people don't come to Ndekezi's house which was very close to the street, and it was too late for us to try to run.

"Open up your house! We want to go in and look around to make sure that you are not hiding anyone!" someone shouted loudly. "I . . . I don't have anyone in the house!" we heard Ndekezi reply. "Just open up, we can't trust you!" was the terse response.

We sat there in the room unable to move, still tightly holding on to each other and praying, when over twenty soldiers, policemen and a few of the Mayor's staff came barging into the house. We could hear the sound of furniture being dragged across the floor as they rummaged through the house, and they quickly reached the room where we were sitting. My hands became cold as I saw them, and my heart raced at about sixty miles an hour. They all carried guns and wore uniforms and had angry looks on their faces. Mom was speechless and shaken, and neither of us moved an inch from where we were sitting. "God if this is our last day, please take our souls to a good place!" I prayed in my heart.

"How could you hide these people here?" asked one of the leaders of the group. "Don't touch these people please! They have suffered enough!" Ndekezi bravely replied. They ignored him, and Deo, the Mayor's communal secretary, looked at us with scorn and anger and started pointing his gun at us. Surprisingly, a policeman named Bavugilije pushed him aside and started speaking in our favor. "Let me tell you, this woman used to be my classmate. She is a good person and was pardoned by some of our colleagues a few days ago. Most of her family has already been killed and she is left only with her little girl. Please let us not kill her. Please! Just leave them alone please!"

Mom and I sat there like statues, surprised but relieved and silently thanking God for coming to our defense once again. Bavugilije continued pleading and insisting to the others that they leave us alone amid loud protests, until Deo shouted: "Let's leave, let's get out of here! Her life is finished anyway!"

I really do not know what motivated Bavugilije to do what he did, but all I can say is that God spoke through him that day! Ndekezi was relieved when they left and we thanked God for sparing us again and felt that He still wanted us to live despite all we'd been through so far. "Don't worry; Allah will protect you no matter what." Ndekezi said to us after they left. He appeared motivated now more than ever to keep hiding us.

The policemen and soldiers continued searching other houses in the community and we could hear the ruckus they were causing as they went from house to house. Ndekezi became worried that they might find six Tutsis who his friend Habayo was hiding in his house. Habayo's house was just across the street and it would only take the group a couple minutes to get to it.

The 'paramilitary' group seemed to be growing in numbers as Interahamwe killers joined their ranks as their searches intensified. They were filled with anger and hatred, and the devil appeared to be working tirelessly within them. I contemplated on the spectacle and others I had seen before, and wondered whether they realized for a moment that we too are human beings and were entitled to the same basic human rights as them.

Minutes later, the sound of people being beaten outside suddenly jolted me out of my meditation. My heart jumped, thinking that some of our people may have been found in the houses they were searching and were being brutalized. Mom and I just looked at each other and started crying!

Suddenly, Laura rushed into the house sobbing: "Oh my God, they just took Habayo and six people they found in his home and have tied them all together and are torturing them outside!" I was crushed in my spirit and I felt it was too much for my mind to absorb. "Some people in the crowd said that they are taking them to the mass grave in Kinihira to torture them and then throw their bodies in!" she added.

We had heard about Kinihira before as it had become infamous in the area because of those horrible killings and torture that they were subjecting people to there.

As Ndekezi's house was so close to the street, we heard people chatting among themselves as they passed by the following day. "That traitor Habayo and the six cockroaches he was hiding were beaten all the way to Kinihira and trampled by soldiers' military boots!" said one passerby jubilantly. "Yeah, and some of their ribs and other body parts were broken as they tortured them to death!" chimed in another. I cried for most of that day, feeling hurt within my heart and asking God to enlighten those misguided people. I felt that they were blinded in their hearts and minds and couldn't see the evil of their behavior. That day was also painful for Ndekezi and many other Muslims in that community. Although he was a Hutu, Habayo was considered a traitor by the killers for hiding those five men and their sister.

That evening Ndekezi sat outside the house talking with some friends, still grieving about what had happened to those Tutsis and his friend Habayo. We were inside sitting as usual when we heard the voice of Patrice, brother of our former 'friend' Leon. "Where is Jeanne?" Patrice shouted, apparently talking to Ndekezi. On hearing this, I whispered: "Mom, I'm hearing Patrice outside asking for you," and she replied "Yes, my child, I heard him too."

Ndekezi did not respond and Patrice became agitated, saying to him: "She should be killed! I don't understand why she wasn't killed yesterday when they found her in your house! I'm going to kill that woman myself!" We then heard Ndekezi raise his voice and say in an angered tone: "Patrice, you're not going to do anything to her and her daughter and if you try, I'll kill you myself." I became very frightened upon hearing the exchanges, but Mom comforted me, saying: "Don't worry my child, just keep praying; do not cease to pray! God will protect us as he has done before, and if anything happens he will receive us with the others!"

By this time, Ndekezi's friends also stood up with him, as we heard them telling him that he should leave and not show up there again. After the exchanges stopped, Ndekezi came into the house and told us that Patrice was armed with a machete but was alone and that he himself had taken up a machete to stand up against him. "I was really angry at the level the situation had reached, and was about to lose my cool with him!" he said to us. We were thankful for his strength and bravery and unwavering commitment to protect us in the face of those challenging situations.

That day I thought about my sister and prayed that God would also protect her wherever she was. Many people were now aware that we were hiding by Ndekezi but somehow the tension directed at us was not as heavy as it was before Officer Bavugilije spared us. The following evening Ndekezi brought two friends we knew from the area, to see us in the house. He brought Alice and her daughter Julienne to us where we were sitting and they told us that they had heard all the stories around about what had been happening to us and wanted to see us and say hello. They showed empathy for what we were going through and said they would keep praying for us in their daily prayers.

Julienne left after speaking to us briefly, saying that she was going to cook something for us. "I know Macwa likes good food, so I brought her some French fries with meat and sauce to make her feel good for now!" she said to us as she returned with the food. I was so happy for that food especially the French fries which I last had in my home more than three months before. What touched me most was to know that someone had thought of me in that way and remembered that I had a life before.

Alice left and returned with a few pieces of clothing which she gave to us. Those clothes we had been using for so long had become tattered and dirty, so it was a welcome change for us. We thanked Alice and Julienne for their genuine compassion, and they prayed for us before leaving for their home. The love they showed to us highlighted another complexity of the cruel genocide, as Julienne's brother Augustin was one of the notorious killers in the area and a major organizer of the genocide. He was known for his extreme cruelty towards his victims, into whose ears, noses and other body parts he inserted nails as a form of torture.

We were now well into the month of June and wondering what was going to happen next. Foreign news stations were reporting that many hundreds of thousands of Tutsis and moderate Hutus had already been killed across the country, and the Interahamwe and other militias were still searching everywhere and killing the few Tutsis that they could find still alive. Those reported numbers made it painfully obvious that very few Tutsis remained. That realization scared me further, knowing how thirsty the Interahamwe were for Tutsi blood. I shuddered at the thought that since they knew where we were hiding, they would return to kill us when they could find no one else to kill. My throat dried up with fear and I started to pray: "Dear God, please help those people to change and open their minds to accept that what they are doing is against your word."

I didn't know how to pray for this at the beginning of the tragedy and tended to tell God to punish them for what they were doing to us. Now, after such painful experiences during those horrific months, my consciousness was renewed. I was now praying for my enemies and felt better inside!

I was becoming very weak physically but was doing my best to be strong mentally. That period of accommodation at Ndekezi's house in the month of June with less running in the bushes helped me to get back some energy and I pushed myself every second to be stronger.

Jeanette was hopefully still with Jonathan's family but we had no news about her at all. I was always thinking and worrying about her and prayed for her safety. One day when Ndekezi came to the room to see us, Mom asked him if he could consider having her stay with us, as we felt more protected for the time being. Ndekezi promptly agreed and told Mom that he would go in search of her by nightfall.

We sat there waiting patiently after he left that evening, looking forward to seeing Jeanette. "Mom, Macwa, I'm here!" she whispered as she walked into the room and saw us. We both burst into tears, happy to see that she was still alive. We hugged each other and cried, and I immediately realized that she was in bad physical shape, almost like a skeleton. We continued to cry, sad about how she looked. "I am sorry Miss Jeanne; I too was shocked when I saw her! I am embarrassed that my friend neglected her so much!" Ndekezi said to Mom.

Laura brought us a bucket of water and Mom and I helped Jeanette to wash herself. She was happy to get rid of the torn and dirty clothes she had, and replace them with the extra piece of clothing which Alice had given us. Laura gave her some food which she could hardly swallow. "My child, what did they do to you?" Mom asked enquiringly. Jeanette told us that while she was at Jonathan's home she was badly mistreated.

"I was hungry most of the time while everyone else was given food, and they all looked at me with scorn," she lamented, choking up with emotion. "They did not allow me to even wash my face, and always spoke to me in a harsh way, yelling at me all the time! I was scared and felt alone, and thought that you all were killed and that made me more scared!" she ended sobbingly. As she talked we were all crying, and the trauma was very visible on her face. Mom held her in her arms to comfort her and said to her: "Don't worry my child, you are with us now, and no matter what happens we will be together!"

★   ★   ★

REFLECTIONS ON CHAPTER 11

There were many types of killings and associated crimes against humanity during the genocide, and I believe that no matter how much the perpetrators try to trivialize the roles they played, they were culpable if such roles fall into any of the categories of participation below.

- There were those who were hunting and killing people— *Those were the hard core killers.*

- There were those in authority who were planning and inciting the killing of innocent people by words, actions and provision of resources—*Those were the masterminds and probably even more culpable than the actual killers.*

- There were those, especially women, who were always watching and spying to know where people were hiding to inform the killers—*Those were killers too in their hearts and minds.*

- There were those who rejected people coming to them for refuge knowing fully well that those persons were in grave danger of being killed—*In my opinion they also supported what was happening, although some of them were fearful that they would also be killed if it was discovered that they were hiding Tutsis.*

We faced all those types of killers wherever we went, but by the grace of God we were not killed even though some of us were hurt in many other ways.

As civilized human beings, we owe it to our own consciences to be extremely vigilant and stand up against any ills that are manifestly wrong in our society. If we all speak with one voice in our condemnation of those ills, the would-be perpetrators will know that they do not have our support and would eventually abandon what they set out to do.

I am grateful to the Muslim community in Rubengera for their brave efforts to protect us and so many others during the genocide.

CHAPTER 12

CONFLICTED RESCUERS

In April, May and the early part of June we had been through "hell on earth" and had managed to cheat death many times through God's grace and a few good hearts. In comparison, those few weeks in Ndekezi's home had been like paradise. Ndekezi's compassion provided us some respite and had started to slowly restore some semblance of our dignity. That small respite may have actually been the light at the end of the tunnel, as by the end of June the RPF had captured parts of the country and were moving to take control of the remaining parts in an effort to halt the killings.

The international community had failed to act, while our defenseless people were unsuccessfully trying to escape from the brutal massacres. The meager resources which the RPF had at their disposal hindered their advance to capture the remaining provinces. With Kibuye being the last to be reached by them, the Interahamwe and other militias continued to be active and were still killing people in our region.

A few days after we heard the good news about the RPF, Alice came bursting into Ndekezi's home filled with excitement. "Have you heard that French soldiers are in the area asking survivors to come to their camps for assistance?" she asked Mom excitedly. "They have camps set up in the Rubengera High School and the Presbyterian Nuns' Convent!" she continued matter-of-factly.

"Are you sure that's what they came here for?" Ndekezi responded with skepticism. "That's what I heard, but I can go to the Nun's Convent and confirm it myself!" Alice replied. She hurried out the door and returned about an hour later and told us that she had spoken with a nun at the convent who confirmed that the French were in fact receiving survivors.

It was said in the news that the French had actually come to assist thousands of Hutus who were fleeing across the border into Congo in fear of reprisals from the RPF for the mass killings they had committed against the Tutsis. In fact, the talk in the area was that the French soldiers were being received by those governmental people in the area who had organized the killings and were still intent on eliminating Tutsis who were still alive.

Ndekezi was still mistrustful of the information Alice had received from the nuns. To satisfy himself, he went to ask a few people around the Rubengera High School about it. He found out that when the French initially arrived there were survivors who had come out of hiding and had gone there thinking they would be rescued by them but were instead taken by Interahamwe from the school and killed as soon as they got there. Ndekezi was troubled by the conflicting information and told us that he didn't trust the French soldiers who were regularly in the company of Interahamwe killers.

Alice kept insisting that we try the Nun's Covent but Ndekezi was not convinced. Mom meanwhile was deep in thought as the two kept arguing about whether we should take the chance to try them or not. "I'm tired of being in hiding knowing that we could be killed anytime!" she said finally. "Besides, going to the nuns is a risk I am prepared to take! We have escaped death so many times, so if we are killed going there it would mean that our time had come. We should go there!" she ended.

Mom had made her decision and Ndekezi had no choice but to concede. He devised a plan to take us there just after nightfall, and promised to get the help of his closest friend Barry to accompany us also. Alice volunteered herself and her daughter Julienne, and promised to get one of her "good" brothers to accompany us.

As we prepared ourselves, Mom said to Jeanette and I: "Kids, our journey is not over yet. We need to keep praying for our safety on the way there and upon our arrival, okay?" as we shook our heads in agreement. The team assigned to accompany us to the Convent all gathered at Ndekezi's house early that evening to await nightfall. Before leaving I prayed and asked God to be with us on this journey and protect us as he always does. Mom, Jeanette and I were ready and eager to go to the Nun's Convent that night!

We left the house and they took us through some back roads to avoid the many Interahamwe roadblocks. As we walked we could hear the killers talking at the Gitikinini shopping center. Although we were walking in the middle of the group and there were many of us, we were still very scared. I remember looking down from the pathway we had followed overlooking the Gitikinini center and saw those killers sitting and talking loudly and really enjoying themselves. I also saw Nsengimana's house in the distance where lots of people were also gathered talking. It was a distasteful scene, especially for us kids who had been so badly threatened and traumatized.

As we approached the convent we saw a guy walking in the opposite direction with a machete in his hand, and, without stopping, Ndekezi casually greeted him, saying: "Hey brother, it looks like you're coming from work! Good job, keep up the good work!" to which the guy replied: "Thanks," and continued on his way. We breathed a sigh of relief and kept on walking briskly, praying that we get to the Convent without meeting anyone else on the street. By the grace of God we arrived there without incident with Ndekezi in the lead. During those three months the killers often referred to their daily activities against the Tutsis as "work."

"Don't say a word; me and Barry will speak to the soldiers in French on your behalf!" Ndekezi warned as we approached the gate. One of the soldiers with a gun in his hand immediately greeted us and asked where we had come from. "These ladies have been hiding for months and are at risk of being killed. They need help from you!" Barry responded.

"Sorry, they will have to go back. We have already received many people and are not taking any more for now!" the soldier said calmly. "Are you sending them to be killed? We met killers on the street and there is no way we can pass again without them being killed!" Barry countered defiantly. The French soldier fell silent for a moment and spoke with another soldier next to him. He then nodded his head indicating that we can come in. "Thank God!" Mom and I sighed as we hurried through the gate with Jeanette, while Ndekezi and his friends smiled and waved us goodbye and headed back home.

As we got inside we were told to sit on the stairs of one of the Nuns' quarters not too far from the gate. As we sat there I thought about the many times I had been to the Convent to buy bread before the genocide begun, and the kindness the nuns used to show me by offering me tea and talking kindly to me. I also reflected on the last time I was able to go there to buy bread when the killings started. I wondered if those Tutsi Nuns that I used to meet there were still alive. Those thoughts took me back to the horrors of the genocide and I had to shake them out of my head, not wanting to relive that pain. As we sat on those stairs waiting to see what next was going to happen, I turned my mind back to the reality of what we may still have to face.

Other survivors were sitting on the other side of the stairs, and from their tattered appearance and visible wounds on their bodies, they had clearly been through a lot of suffering like we had. Among them was a young girl who lived next door to Grandma Felicite. Mom approached her and asked if she had any information about her mom. "Oh, Miss Jeanne, I am happy to see you, but . . . but . . . I'm sorry to tell you that Neighbor Felicite was killed during the carnage," she sobbed. Mom immediately broke down in tears, and Jeanette and I held on to her with sadness and also started to cry.

Moments later, before our tears had subsided, the French soldier who had allowed us in motioned to us in sign language which we understood to mean that we will move out of that camp to another place. Mom and I quickly tried to wipe our tears away and looked at each other, fearing that they might have planned something that was not good for us. We, however, tried to remain calm and hoped for the best, not sure of what to expect from them.

After a few minutes they signaled us to board a truck which was parked outside the gate which we did. They drove away and we had no idea where they were taking us! No one spoke, and after driving for about twenty minutes we arrived at the Rwimpiri Primary School. This school was among the most neglected in the area and was situated in a remote area without electricity or running water. As we alighted from the truck we saw a few other survivors who were already there. We felt a bit relieved on seeing them and were happy that there was no sign of Interahamwe in the area. We moved around looking at the survivors to see whether there was anyone we knew, and were pleasantly surprised when we came upon one of our cousins Immaculee, who we had not heard about since the genocide started, and were not aware that she was still alive.

We all screamed with joy upon seeing each other and hugged together and started to cry, overcome with emotion and not knowing what else to say. No words were coming out, only tears as we looked at the condition of each other. That moment was very emotional for all of us and this was the first family member we had seen except for our cousin Chantal who we had met a few weeks earlier.

The physical appearance of all of us had changed a lot because of hiding without food or drink for excessively long periods, little or no showers or change of clothing, and unable to comb our hair or brush our teeth. We had all lost a lot of weight, but I was worse than everybody else as my body was very weak and my energy level was very low. Most, if not all of the survivors we met may have lost a lot of weight and looked so haggard and broken that it was not easy to recognize some of those we had known before.

We sat down on the rocky ground outside in the moon light with Immaculee, as there was very few "furniture" or other resources at the school. As we sat, we started slowly asking each other about what difficulties were faced in getting to the French camp. It was not very easy to talk about our ordeal, as we were still very fragile. The conversation was actually between Mom and Immaculee, as Jeanette and I were much affected by what had happened to us and kept quiet trying to deal with the weakness in our bodies and minds. For me I was not feeling myself and felt like I was in another world and was getting flashbacks in my mind from time to time.

Mom and Immaculee conversed for a little while in the midst of a lot of tears, and it appeared that they also were not able to talk much about their ordeal just yet. The only burning issue for them at that point was to know whether there were any other family members who might still be alive.

"I only know about Chantal who may still be alive, as we saw her about three weeks ago in the midst of the chaos! I pray that she has survived but I am not sure whether anything had happened to her since then," Mom told Immaculee. At that point in time none of them were able to speak about our ordeals. The painful memories were still too fresh and intense, especially the unwarranted loss of family members who were near and dear to us. They were both crying throughout as they spoke and it was really painful for all of us.

Jeanette and I sat there motionless, torn between the joy of seeing our cousin and the horrors of what we had been through. The pain within me was so intense that I didn't know how to feel or respond in a normal way about anything anymore. Even now I sometimes remember those horrible moments of my life and am moved to tears when I recall those periods of our deep pain and suffering, as young kids who were not supposed to go through those things.

After a few minutes we started looking at additional survivors in the camp to see whether we knew any of them. Some of them were wounded while others were weak and frail and had difficulty moving around. We moved around within and outside the classrooms and found some people we knew. We also came across a woman who had many severe wounds on one side of her body and could hardly move. She was there with her husband who was a Hutu and who was taking care of her wounds. He seemed deeply hurt about his wife's condition and committed himself to be there for her.

Although I had my own physical and emotional pain, it was heartbreaking for me to see the condition that some of the other survivors there were in. As we walked, we met a mother and some of her children who were friends of our family. Mom embraced them and they cried together, overcome with emotion and unable to say anything to each other. One of the kids, Florence, who was older than me, held on tightly to Jeanette and I and looked at us in disbelief at how frail we had become. She tried to comfort us amid an avalanche of tears. I talked with Florence for a while but Jeanette was very quiet and appeared not yet able to respond to anything she was asked.

Florence showed much concern for us younger kids who were there. She tried to comfort us, offering us crackers and soup which the French had made available. She appeared very strong in mind and showed genuine empathy for us, and her actions belied the fact that she herself had been through rough times in hiding during the genocide.

Finding a place to sleep was difficult and some of the survivors slept on the few chairs and tables that were available, while others slept on the ground. We tried to stick together as a group in that small school, and when we started feeling sleepy, we laid our skeleton bodies on the stony dirt ground which was painful and uncomfortable. Some of the wounded survivors could not lie down on the hard surfaces because of the type of wounds they had, and tried to sit instead. Deep hurt and emotional pain was evident in the eyes and faces of every one of us survivors who were gathered there.

After about two days there, we were elated to see our cousin Chantal being brought to the camp. I remember seeing her walking on the playing field towards us and we all ran to embrace her in tears, happy that she was alive. She had also lost a lot of weight and looked so much different.

A few days later, the French announced that they would be taking some of us to a better place but had not yet decided who would go and who would stay. For me, I was not yet trusting of the French and was still afraid of them handing us over to the Interahamwe. Their decision that some of us would go and others stay therefore scared me to death. To our relief, they finally decided that all of us would go except a few who were helping them receive other survivors and document their information. Immaculee was among those chosen to stay to help them, something she had already been doing since she arrived at the camp. The rest of us had to leave, so we said goodbye to her amid tears of course, and boarded the truck and departed towards Kibuye Town.

The Interahamwe roadblocks were still in operation at many points along the way. They allowed the French military vehicles through without checking inside, but we were all very scared to hear them still spewing out their hate speech and worse yet, to actually see their faces and be so close to them as we passed concealed in the trucks. We managed to get through the roadblocks uneventfully and arrived at the Eto High School where the camp was set up.

We greeted survivors as we walked by, looking for anyone known to us. Most of the survivors there were strangers from different parts of the province and many of them had large open wounds over their bodies which were unattended and looked horrible. I remember getting close to a young woman named Francoise who turned out to be the daughter of a couple who Mom knew. Her previously beautiful face was disfigured with wounds all over and one could tell that she was tortured. We all greeted each other and Mom spoke to her and hugged her.

I was deeply saddened by how Francoise looked and imagined the pain she was in, but could not find any words to say to her. Despite her obvious pain and suffering, she still talked with kids and others around with a smile on her face. Looking at her made me feel mentally strong even though my physical weakness persisted.

As we continued to walk, we came across a few other people we knew from our area, including a Hutu woman named Charlotte and her Tutsi fiancé Epaphrodite. We hugged and exchanged greetings with them. Mom was somehow surprised to see Charlotte but thought that she might have gone through hard times like some other Hutus who had supported their Tutsi partners or spouses and had become targets also.

They moved to a corner and sat down to talk with Mom for a while and they told her what had happened to them. I was very proud of Charlotte who did not allow the bad things her people were doing to Tutsis to change the way she felt about her fiancé, and maintained the good heart which she always had.

As we moved to survey others sitting around, we saw orphaned kids, heartbroken widows and just a few men who were lucky to have escaped the killings. Very few of the people there were fortunate to have any significant amount of family members remaining, and deep pain was evident within each person.

The Eto school camp was in better shape than Rwimpiri and we were able to sit and sleep on cemented floors of the classrooms instead of the rocky dirt floor. We had been given only one blanket for four of us to lie down on, so sleeping was still uncomfortable. There were many Christians among us in the classroom where we slept. They worshipped, cried and sang gospel songs and kept praying all the time and I joined in the activities from where I lay down. Some of them talked about their experiences and it was disheartening to hear stories of cruelty, suffering and survival that were in some cases much more horrific than ours. Those resilient people were trying to sing and pray to God who was our only refuge for easing our severely wounded hearts.

Some kids of my age group sometimes walked around the compound looking for other kids to talk with to ease their pain. Most times I couldn't join them as I felt weaker and weaker as time went by. Apart from my physical weakness, I felt like my mind was also in deep depression and I had to keep telling myself that I was okay and will continue to be okay no matter what. I needed to feel a little better on the inside in order to overcome whatever was showing on the outside.

Sometimes I pushed myself to walk but Mom insisted that I stay in one place, fearing I would faint due to my low energy level. I continually asked God to help me and I put my entire trust in him. I tried eating the crackers the French gave to us, but was not able to as I kept throwing up all the time. Mom encouraged me to eat, but I couldn't keep anything in my stomach for long. The only thing that helped was when I drank some tea that the French gave us which was not much, given that their initial mission in Rwanda did not cater for providing food and shelter for us.

"That's Chouchou! That's Chouchou!" I shouted with joy, as Aunt Esperance emerged from a vehicle with other survivors. It was just two days after we arrived at Eto High School and a jubilant moment for us. We had not heard any news about her since the start of the genocide and were thankful to God when we saw her. We were all crying with joy and sadness at the same time as she had also changed much and looked very thin, and her clothes were badly wrinkled.

"Thank God you are alive! I didn't know whether anyone of you were still alive!" she shouted, as we hugged together in tears. We held her hands and took her to where we were staying in one of the classrooms and sat down with her. "Why does Macwa look so much weaker and frailer than Chantal and Jeanette?" she asked Mom as she looked tearfully at me. "She has been very weak for some time and I'm worried about her!" Mom replied.

Aunt Esperance related to us what she had gone through and where she had been hiding. As expected, the exchange of our horror stories added to all of our pain, so it was too much to relive all at one time. My aunt told us that she hid under very difficult circumstances and the killers came mere inches from finding her on many occasions but by the grace of God they didn't. "At the beginning of the genocide I was moving around in the bushes when I heard some kids saying there are cockroaches in the bushes near them! I became terrified when I heard them running away screaming and feared they would call some killers!" she related. The kids did in fact call the killers who came searching around those bushes and passed where she was sitting holding her breath, but they did not see her.

Aunt Esperance also related to us that about a week after the problem started, on April 15 to be exact, while in the bushes she heard passersby saying that some killers had found her mother hiding in a neighbor's home and dragged her onto the street and killed her. That same day she also heard people talking and saying that Ngoga was chased by a large group of people who caught up with him in the bushes and killed him.

Aunt Esperance told us that she was devastated by those news that day but in order to survive she had to shake off her emotions and try to be strong. She kept hiding from place to place in the bush near our area for more than a month with little or no food to eat. Things were getting worse, so she sought refuge at the homes of different people she knew, most of whom turned her down. An old friend Cecile eventually hid her behind her fire pit in her old kitchen, where she stayed undetected for over two months. Killers came on several occasions and searched everywhere including the kitchen and pushed the firewood around but luckily did not find her.

One night in early July Cecile told her about the French soldiers who had come into the region and that they were taking survivors into their camps. When she heard that, she was relieved about the prospect of not having to lie down under those piles of firewood much longer and told Cecile that she would go there.

The night before they planned to leave, Cecile felt ashamed to let her go the way she was looking and boiled water for her to take a bath, which was the first time she had one in the three months she had been in hiding. She also boiled her clothes in hot water to get rid of some of the lice and dirt that had accumulated in them.

Amid tears, Aunt Esperance blurted out to us: "That's why you see my clothes are so horribly wrinkled like they were chewed by a cow because of being boiled for a long time!" She also told us that Cecile had related to her that the killers had taken us to so many places, and she was worried that she might not find any of us alive.

During the time Aunt Esperance was conversing, I wasn't talking or participating in any of the conversation. I was in my own world and lay down in one spot getting flashbacks about the time we were in hiding, especially the night my body was violated. Those images were constantly in my head, and I did not feel normal either physically or mentally. I wasn't able to open up and tell my aunt what had happened to me. I was at a stage where I couldn't relate anything yet to anyone about what had happened.

We had been at the Eto Kibuye High School for a few days when the French told us they would be taking us to the RPF camp which was not very far from where we were. At first we were afraid, as none of us were aware that the RPF had reached Kibuye. I thought the French didn't want to keep us any longer and were going to drop us at the Interahamwe roadblocks. Despite our fears, however, we had no choice but to accept to go as we were squarely in their hands.

We trusted in God to be with us throughout that journey as they packed us all into trucks and headed towards Gitarama. Some of us were frightened as we passed through Kibuye Town, and I remember looking through some openings at the back of the truck and saw those Interahamwe on the streets still armed with machetes, spears and all sorts of weapons they had been using to kill people during the past months. "We will make sure the RPF don't find any cockroaches alive when they reach Kibuye!" they chanted as we approached hidden in the trucks.

I could detect some defeat in their tone, but they were still full of hate in their minds. It was very scary for me to look at them again and to hear what they were saying. All the survivors in the truck were scared and some of us did not think that we would make it through. At that moment we prayed so hard within our hearts to be able to pass them and reach where the RPF was camping.

"Sorry, we can't go any further and we have to return to the camp!" one of the soldiers shouted from the front of the truck about half mile away from the RPF camp. "You should keep moving on foot from here until you reach the RPF who are located straight ahead!" added the soldier, with finality in his tone. It was around midday and we found ourselves in the middle of a dangerous place! The French had dropped us in a sort of "no man's land" between the last Interahamwe checkpoint and one of the RPF's military posts. They drove off before we even had the RPF camp in sight, and we panicked, fearing that we would be killed by the Interahamwe if they saw us. We all started to pray to God to help us reach the RPF camp before the killers could see us, and moved as fast as we could, following the directions the French had given us.

Some of the stronger survivors tried to help those wounded ones by holding their arms and helping them along. As we walked we could see the killers through the trees in the distance talking loudly but we had agreed that no one should run, so as to avoid attracting their attention. I don't know how I got my energy back but I was moving as fast as the others and keeping up with them. The only thing in my mind was to reach to the RPF and only then I would take a moment to breathe once again!

★   ★   ★

REFLECTIONS ON CHAPTER 12

It is ironic that the French military came to Rwanda on a mission to primarily provide humanitarian help to the very perpetrators of the genocide as they fled across borders to neighboring countries, while no one saw our plight as being urgent enough to intervene.

By some unclear twist of fate, those French soldiers may have been deeply moved by the horror being committed against us which they saw firsthand upon their arrival. They started providing partial shelter to survivors who could reach their camps, from where they would convey them as close as they could to the nearest RPF location.

What they were doing for us may have been in conflict with their mission to provide humanitarian assistance to the fleeing Hutus, and may have come about due to the humane hearts of many of them who were personally touched by what they had seen when they landed on Rwandan soil. The fact that they could not hand us over directly to the RPF spoke for itself and left a bittersweet taste in our mouths. Nevertheless, we are grateful for what those French soldiers did for us, as their assistance did help save some lives in our area.

Me and my siblings a few months before the start of the genocide.
I'm second from the right holding baby brother Bon Fils, with sister
Jeanette on my left and brothers Philbert and Pascal to my right.

Aunt Esperance near Mom's flower garden in 1997.

PART III

NEW BEGINNINGS

No matter how big your problem is,
God is bigger,
No matter how intense fear is,
Love dissolves it,
No matter who you are,
You matter always and forever."

Marianne Williamson

★　★　★

Chapter 13

TRUE SAVIORS

The Interahamwe did not see us, and after walking for about twenty minutes we reached safely to a place called Rambura. As we approached that village, we saw a small primary school just ahead of us with some soldiers in military uniforms in the compound. "There's the RPF camp! We're safe! We're safe!" shouted several survivors. I looked at the soldiers and knew they were RPF soldiers by the physical makeup of most of them. I immediately felt relieved even though we didn't speak to any of them as yet.

We continued walking towards the soldiers and they waved us on with welcoming gestures and a friendly attitude. They were appalled to see the condition many of us were in at the time and immediately tried to put us at ease. "Where were you during the genocide?" and "How were you able to reach here?" were some of the questions they started to ask us. We responded to their questions and briefly explained some of the horrors we had been through and the situation that still existed with Interahamwe roadblocks. We also told them that we were very happy to see them, and had feared that we would be killed on our way to their camp!

"You don't need to worry anymore! You are in the safest place now and you won't be hurt by anyone again!" said one of the officers in a fatherly tone. I thanked God for being with us throughout and delivering us safely to the RPF. I also took the time to thank God for helping them through the difficult mission they had undertaken on our behalf to stop the horrible killings which had taken the lives of so many innocent people!

The soldiers took us into the school and told us to find a comfortable place to sit and relax our bodies. It was very comforting to be spoken to and treated as a human being by our fellow Rwandans once more. The school was similar in condition to the one at Rwimpiri. I didn't care about its physical condition or lack of amenities, as I now had some joy in my heart and felt blessed to see friendly soldiers who had come to save us from those horrible people who wanted to kill us all.

The soldiers cooked a meal for us while we sat and talked with some of them, feeling safe for the first time in more than three months! They showed deep empathy for us as they listened to some of our horror stories. Many of them had more than likely lost a number of their family members but they still had work to do to capture the remaining parts of the country before they could find time to check on the status of their own families. It was difficult for them but they were determined to keep fighting for peace and make our country better. They were very brave and committed and their strength was beyond amazing.

We were about twenty people there and everyone was looking forward to eating some decent hot food for a change. When the food came I tried to eat as everyone else but I could only eat a little at a time. I was very weak and my stomach had shrunk. "Are you guys okay?" some soldiers asked, checking up on us as we ate. We relaxed for a while after the meal and several others came to us individually and asked how we were feeling and wanted to know how we had managed to avoid being discovered.

"I can tell how much you have suffered, but tell me . . . . How did you manage to hide from those killers for so long?" one soldier asked me enquiringly. "I have not lived through the genocide but have seen its deadly aftermath as we moved from province to province driving out the army and civilian militias and took over control," he added.

For most of us, it was difficult at the onset to relate to them what we had gone through, especially those of us who had been sexually assaulted. The events had been so extreme that it was still very painful to talk about our stories in detail so soon. 'I . . . I'm sorry, it's too much for me to talk about right now," I said to the soldier, with tears streaming down my face. "Oh, don't worry, it's okay . . . I know how difficult it is for all of you!" he said, as he gently held my shoulder, obviously mindful of the pain and trauma within me. The soldier was still talking to me as I held my head down, trying to wipe away the tears.

"Paul, Paul! How are you?" I said, as I lifted my head and recognized another soldier walking by. "Macwa, is that you?" he replied, his face lighting up in disbelief as he stooped down to embrace me. We had not seen each other for many years, so we started talking. The soldier who was previously talking to me politely excused himself and left. I felt comfortable talking to Paul, telling him that Mom and the others had also survived and were at the camp.

"Thank God some of you survived! I have heard that some of my own family members and many of our neighbors were killed," he said sadly. "I'm so sorry to hear that! It has been such a tragedy for all of us!" I replied, trying to console him. "Let me take you to see Mom and the others!"

Paul was happy to see Mom, Aunt Esperance, Chantal and Jeanette, and warmly embraced each of them as he said: "It's so good to see some of my neighbors alive! I have heard that so many people have been killed in our area!" As we talked, he related to us the story about how he joined RPF.

"In 1990 I was a FAR soldier and my battalion launched an attack on the RPF near the Ugandan border. I was shot in an exchange of gunfire, and my own FAR colleagues shot me themselves as they fled from the advancing RPF and abandoned me there to die!" he related to us sadly.

"So how did you manage to be fighting with RPF?" Mom asked him in earnest. "Fortunately for me the RPF soldiers found me as I lay bleeding and captured me and took me to their camp where they treated my injuries!" he replied, adding: "They treated me like one of their own so when the time came for an exchange of POW's I refused to rejoin the FAR and stayed with the RPF to help them fight their cause."

Paul, who was Hutu, ended by saying: "Thank God we were able to come back to our country to help the remaining survivors! We will do all we can to protect you against this happening again!"

127

While he was talking to us, Paul kept looking at me and when he was finished he pulled me aside and said: "You look in much worse shape than your little sister and cousin. Apart from the starvation and bad treatment you all endured, did you undergo any grave torture at the hands of the Interahamwe?"

I immediately started to cry and told him: "Yes they did bad stuff to me." He placed one arm across my shoulders and asked with concern: "I hope they did not rape you like they did to so many others, did they? Still in tears and unable to speak, I nodded my head in the affirmative.

"Oh no, how could those monsters do such a thing to a child? Don't worry, you'll be taken care of and they will be punished for what they have done!" I guess he probably saw something different in my countenance that I couldn't realize myself, as he was the first person to directly ask me that question!

"Miss Jeanne, I am sorry to know that poor Macwa was robbed of her innocence in the most violent way at such a tender age! She will need a lot of support from you to help her through the psychological trauma she must be going through!" Paul said to Mom seriously. Before leaving, he promised Mom and Aunt Esperance that he will make sure that we are fine during our stay there. Holding me in his arms which I needed so much at the time, he said to me: "Macwa, be strong and don't worry anymore . . . you will be fine and we are with you . . . okay?" His words and actions towards me made me feel better inside. Without knowing it, Paul had momentarily filled the void left by Dad's death, and I saw him as a big brother who really cared!

After several days in the RPF camp in Rambura, we had to move to Ruhango, another town in the Gitarama province as it was called then. They wanted us to be in a safer environment further away from the areas not yet captured by them. They also wanted to provide us with slightly better accommodation, including normal showers and change of clothing which we badly needed. We were all happy at the prospect of moving for those reasons.

"We have to make several trips as we only have one small pickup truck!" shouted a soldier to the group lined up outside as scheduled the next morning. We waited patiently with our meager belongings as the truck made several trips back and forth. My family and I were placed on the last trip. Several tall, thin and friendly looking RPF soldiers waved us through to a little "village" in Ruhango and gave us a warm welcome as we hopped out of the pickup truck. It was a different atmosphere in that area, and it gave me a positive feeling that it was the place where we can all begin to recover from the many traumatic events we had endured.

"You will be housed there temporarily!' one of the ranking soldiers told us as he pointed to a large house nearby. "It is not fully habitable but is large enough to accommodate your family and a few other surviving families for the moment," he added. The house was well built and one could tell that it was previously well maintained. Its' windows and doors were missing, however, and some of the walls were damaged. Despite the damage, it was like a castle to us and gave us a sense of freedom at last.

"You can get some food and other basic stuff from the administration office over there!" one soldier told us as he pointed to a nearby building. We were thankful for being there and for whatever they had to give us, as the most important thing for us at the time was peace and security. Two soldiers walked us to the administration office to be officially registered and helped us gather the things we needed to use for a few days.

The missing doors and windows of the house posed a slight challenge for us as it was sometimes windy and cold, so some of the stronger survivors managed to go out and found some wooden boards which they used to block the windows and the door entrance.

"By the way, what will we sleep on tonight?" one lady asked as soon as the makeshift doors and windows were in place. There was no furniture in the house and no mattresses were available for us as yet, so we had to become creative!

The twenty of us assigned to our new 'home' went out in search of banana leaves and found enough for all of us to sleep on. Everyone was thankful for those 'beds' and I remember distinctly how we all joked about it after we finished setting them up, saying "We are rich, we got beds!" None of us had a problem to sleep like that, for what mattered most was that we were secure.

That first day at Ruhango gave us the feeling that the drama of us being hunted was truly over. We were finally free to sit outside and talk and go inside the house to sleep whenever we wished! We actually spent a lot of time sitting outside on the stairs talking, trying to get some fresh air and engage in conversations about different things, which we badly needed to refresh our minds and bodies.

As the days passed, Chantal and Jeanette joined others in walking around the town to explore the area, but I was still weak and not feeling myself, so I used to sit on the stairs outside and watch people walk freely on the streets, grateful for that change in our situation. It was around that time that I started to experience fainting spells from time to time and I wasn't able to control it.

"That's why I don't want you walking around with the others," Mom told me after my first fainting spell. "Don't worry, your aunt and I will be around you all the time, as we do not know how serious your situation could be!" she added.

Unfortunately, there was no medical help available yet so they had to take whatever precautions they could. Mom got some vitamin and mineral-rich food supplements from the administration office which they gave to me and I gradually started to regain my strength. I was happy for that as I needed to explore and feel the freedom of walking on the street once more.

From what Jeanette and Chantal told me, there were still a lot of bodies strewn in some places but I didn't mind, as I had to experience that feeling of freedom myself! I was amazed to see so many people walking around without fear with no one bothering them. It was a good feeling to meet people from other parts of the country who had survived, and converse freely with them.

Weeks went by and a few more survivors were brought to join us. One of them was a young lady named Adrie whose family was our neighbor for many years. "Adrie, Adrie! Is that you?" I called out to greet her as soon as I saw her arrive. "Yes Consolee, it's me, and thank

God you are alive!" she shouted as she ran towards me and the others. We hugged and cried and took her into the house.

"I am lucky to be alive. I have found out that most, if not all of my family have been killed," Adrie said sadly after she settled down. We chatted for a while and as she spoke my heart became full as I reflected on how so many of our families, good friends and neighbors had become part of the massive statistics of those killed. We comforted each other and promised to help one another to cope as much as we could.

"Hey Consolee, you need to cheer up, ma Cherie! We can't let our problems affect our spirit!" Adrie smilingly said to me as I sat staring into space after a while. Like an older sister, she could see my pain and managed to make me smile. "Thanks for cheering me up, Adrie!" I said to her.

It was difficult to sustain my cheerful mood, as I started to fear that I might be infected with the HIV virus as a result of Shinani's sexual assault. Having heard so many bad stories about the virus, I was fearful that if I was infected, I would wither away and die for sure.

I prayed over and over in my heart asking God to "please take away those nagging thoughts from my mind!" Sometimes those fearful thoughts would shift to haunting images of my young innocent brothers and my father being murdered, and recalling those horrific moments prevented me from sleeping well. It was very difficult for me to handle within myself but I leaned on prayer. I kept praying constantly as prayer was helping me get through my day.

"Don't worry, things will be fine and you are going to be like every other girl!" I convinced myself as I tried desperately to transform the negative thoughts that were hurting my spirit into positive ones! Every time those painful thoughts came I sought to prevent myself from being a mental slave of the hurtful things that had happened to me. I didn't want those thoughts to control me . . . . I wanted to control them!

"Kids, the RPF is looking for adult high school graduates to participate in a two month trauma course in Kibingo. What do you think of that?" Mom asked enquiringly one day. "What are the benefits Mom?" I quickly asked. "The training will prepare participants to help survivors deal with their trauma! I think it would be good if I go!" Mom answered with a half smile.

"But Mom, Kibingo is some distance away and there is no transport system. How would you be able to go back and forth for two months?" Jeanette chimed in.

"Don't worry my children . . . this will help us cope with our burdens! I will stay in the training camp for the two months and your Aunt will take care of you while I'm gone!"

It was obvious that Mom's mind was already made up, and she convinced us that the training would help us all. The following day we hugged and bid her farewell together with nine of our housemates. "We'll visit you whenever we could!" we all shouted as they drove away. The very next day Chantal, Jeanette and some others in the house went to visit them at the training camp, but I stayed behind with Aunt Esperance.

"Chou Chou! Macwa! You would not believe what Mom was wearing today!" Chantal shouted as she and Jeanette came running through the open front doorway that evening. "Mom was in uniform and wearing trousers! You should have seen how funny she looked in those pants!" they both chuckled, cracking up with laughter. Aunt Esperance and I couldn't resist joining in the fun they were having at Mom's expense!

I was very happy for Mom to be there, as she had been through so much during that period of genocide. She had to carry us through the bushes from place to place and had seen the love of her life hunted down and killed and her three baby sons led away like lambs to be slaughtered! She also had to deal with the horror of seeing me dragged away by a crazed killer armed with a sword, only to return bruised and bleeding from a violent sexual attack. Those things were heartbreaking for her and she needed to be in a place where she can get help and heal. After the two month training period was completed, all of us in the house were anxious to see Mom and the others return, and curious to know what had transpired during training.

"It was a great experience and the training was very therapeutic for all of us!" beamed the self-appointed spokesman, as the group of us sat down to listen. "The training was necessary to begin the reversal of the bad teachings given to people by misguided leaders for so long! It also taught us many lessons that would help us to reshape the country and live our daily lives better in the future!" added one widow.

The group lauded the presenters for their wisdom in keeping their focus on re-affirming people's consciousness that we are all the same and needed to learn to live together with human dignity and respect for one another, and not on revenge. This was a clear sign to me that our 'saviors' were determined to rebuild the country and do what was right for its citizens. It also made me hopeful that our country would rise above that historic catastrophe and that our young generation would be able to live together with unity, equality and respect. Mom told us that she was happy to have participated, and the experience had changed her thinking somewhat and healed some parts of her inner self that were severely wounded.

With so many 'prospective clients' living in that house, our new "trauma healers" needed to get to work immediately. Their first patient was a widow who had survived with two of her little girls. She was in deep emotional pain and would often awake in the middle of the night screaming. She had been repeatedly raped during the genocide and had lost most of her family. Maria appeared to be 'losing her marbles' and would often say that life meant nothing to her and she did not know why she was still alive. The trauma healers in the house worked tirelessly on her, practicing their newly acquired skills, which seemed to partially help Maria get through her emotional pain over time.

Our stay in Ruhango had been very helpful in so many ways and gave some of us a glimmer of hope for life and the beginning of a desire to move on. As time went by, things were starting to change in the country. The threats were fading with the mass exodus of Interahamwe and other perpetrators fleeing over the border into the Democratic Republic of Congo and other neighboring countries. This gave us great hope and a welcome feeling of peace and security, and it was very clear that the new government was moving to restore some semblance of normalcy in the lives of people and rebuild our country.

"What plans do you have for yourself when the time comes for us to leave Ruhango?" Mom asked Adrie one day. "You have no surviving family members, you should think about coming with us!" she added. "I have not given it any thought Miss Jeanne! I'll think about it and let you know!" Adrie replied.

Later that day we were delighted when Adrie told Mom that she had decided to stay with us. I was excited about the prospect and openly showed it. "I will be happy to continue being your big sister Macwa! You guys are the only 'family' I have now, and I'm happy for that!" Adrie said to me with a broad smile.

Adrie was happy that at least she was with people she knew so well, especially as she considered Mom as an aunt. Even though she tried to be strong we could tell that she was deeply affected by what she had been through. We were happy to be with her and Mom was constantly reassuring her that she would be okay. In the aftermath of the genocide, having someone to be there for you was a form of relief because being alone added to the trauma we were carrying. I was thankful that Mom was there for all of us to help put our lives back together, and my heart went out to those who were less fortunate, especially young orphaned kids.

★   ★   ★

REFLECTIONS ON CHAPTER 13

Members of the Rwandan Patriotic Army were true saviors who liberated us from certain extermination had they not come to our rescue. The speed at which the massacres were being committed and the strategies being employed by the perpetrators to seek out and eliminate every living Tutsi they could find, would have been accomplished had it not been for the intervention of those brave men and women who took up our cause and sacrificed their lives for us.

The Rwandan people must be truly grateful to them and their leaders for their unselfish commitment and the competence they displayed in bringing the vicious genocide to an end and saving the lives of the remaining survivors. Their efforts and dedication to the preservation of life should never be forgotten.

CHAPTER 14

HOMEWARD BOUND

By early to mid July 1994 the RPF had succeeded in taking over control of the entire country and was moving ahead with the daunting task of restoring what they could from the devastation. A great percentage of Interahamwe and other perpetrators of the genocide were fleeing the country, but some of them had stayed behind thinking that they could cover the crimes they had committed. Some of them moved from areas they had lived before to other areas where they were not known, to avoid recognition for what they had done in their home areas.

This situation made it troubling for some of us survivors, not knowing how we would react if we came face to face with killers who were still mingling among us. And yes, such a possibility was very real! Many of those who fled were afraid of facing justice for what they had done, but some were brazen enough to stay. Among those who stayed was a small percentage that did not associate themselves with the killers in any way.

Mom and Aunt Esperance sat discussing this and other things in general with us one evening as we prepared ourselves for an imminent departure from Ruhango. "We don't have a livable home, but the land is still there which we can work on to get a roof over our heads!" said Mom as we tried to discourage her from taking us back to Rubengera.

"If we go anywhere else we'll have nothing to make a start!" Aunt Esperance chimed in. "But Mom . . . Chouchou, we don't want to see that place anymore! They hurt us enough there and it's hard to face them again! I am scared to go back and relive those bad memories of what happened to us!" I replied, trying to dissuade them.

The training Mom had recently taken appeared to have shaped her perspective about going back home and may have aided in making up her mind. She was determined now more than ever to return home to live no matter what.

"Going back to Rubengera which we are familiar with, will give us an advantage! We need to be there so that the perpetrators would realize that we are alive despite their selfish attempts at exterminating us as a people! We will show them that we are no longer afraid of them!" she insisted.

Adrie, our new "family member" was the one to finally persuade us to return home. She said to us: "Your Mom is correct! Don't worry, we will fight to overcome our fears and God will be there with us in everything we do!" We listened, and reluctantly agreed with 'the older heads' that it was the right choice to make. They were happy that we finally came on board and Mom said to us: "Children, continue to be strong and always put God first in everything and he will be there to see us through!"

A few days later, we started to prepare ourselves for our trip back home. Some of the survivors staying in the house had already started to leave, while arrangements were made with an orphanage and some good hearted people in the area to care for some of the orphaned children. When our time came to leave, the RPF brought a vehicle to take us to Kibuye and promised that they would find us a temporary place to stay when we get there.

They drove us along the main road to Kibuye, and as we passed through Rubengera we could see that only pieces of broken walls of our home were still standing. We could also see the spot where my grandparents' home once stood, as well as the home of one of my uncles. Looking up the hills I could see so many homes of friends and colleagues of my parents which had been reduced to rubble. Those images fogged up my brain and I had difficulty breathing when I saw them again.

We did not stop in Rubengera and kept going towards Kibuye Town and came to a stop about forty five minutes later. "Come this way!!" A soldier shouted as he directed us to a building where some basic social services were being provided to returning survivors. "We will give you a few items of foodstuff and help you find temporary shelter!" said another soldier as we alighted from the vehicle in front of the building.

After briefly registering us, the soldiers took us to some unfurnished houses that were slightly damaged, and gave us food and some blankets. We joined some other survivors in one of the houses and introduced ourselves to each other. The sharing arrangement was an improvement from the house we had occupied in Ruhango, as each family was given separate rooms from other survivors.

"My wonderful teacher, I am so happy to see you, I thank God you are alive!" said a voice on the street as Mom stepped outside the house a few hours later. "Nancy, I have not seen you for so many years since I left the Vocational Training School!" replied Mom. She warmly embraced Mom and talked to us for a while and then said she had to leave.

"I'm going to get you all a few things to use in the house! I know what you must have gone through!" Nancy told Mom as she hurried across the street to her home. Nancy was a Hutu woman who was there throughout the genocide. She seemed to be a good person, as I could see in her eyes that she genuinely felt sad for what had happened. About an hour later we heard a knock on the door.

"I brought you some plates, spoons, and some other little stuff that I know you would need to use in the house!" she told Mom as she opened to let her in. Nancy talked to us for a while and we cooked and ate together. A few days passed and we began to get acclimatized to our new surroundings. It was then that I started to feel a little better and my appetite began to improve. I also felt the urge to go outside.

"I feel strong now and would like to go out and walk around with you!" I said to Chantal, Jeanette and Adrie as they prepared to go around Kibuye Town. "Macwa, are you sure?" Chantal queried. "I'm fine, let's go!" I bragged, as we walked onto the street. As we walked, we came upon many destroyed homes, and the stench of rotted bodies was everywhere! It was very depressing and I could feel the sadness all around.

"I wonder if we will be able to be happy and live a normal life again!" I mused, as we ambled along the street. It was difficult to imagine how our future would be.

As we walked through that area we hardly met anyone we knew. The people we started seeing were some of those who had been forced into exile since 1959 and onwards, and were now happy to return home despite the carnage the fleeing killers had left behind. A number of young adults and children born to exiled parents were coming to Rwanda with their parents for the first time.

Macwa! Chantal! "I need to talk to you about something!" said Adrie to us a few days later. "What . . . what is it Adrie?" I asked curiously. "I think I have changed my mind about going to live in Rubengera! I would like to stay here in Kibuye Town and try my luck at getting a job and restarting my life here!" she said decidedly. We really wanted her to come with us but had no choice but to respect her wish.

Mom did not want us to stay too long in Kibuye Town, as her plan was to go back to Rubengera as soon as possible. She left for Rubengera the next day, to assess the situation and explore the possibility of getting a place for us to stay there, while we anxiously awaited her return.

"Guess what? You guys may not believe it, but I found a place where we can stay in Rubengera!" Mom blurted out as she entered the house later that evening. "Really? Please tell us you are not kidding, Mom!" I insisted. "No, Macwa, it's true! I went to our old friend Faustin's home and he and Rachel were elated to see me! They had heard about the many incidents where we were almost killed, but wasn't sure whether we had survived!"

"So how did you manage to get a place for us to stay, Mom?" I asked, impatiently. "God is still opening doors for us my dear!" Let me tell you—before I could have asked, Faustin said to me: "Jeanne, you and your husband have been good friends and clients to us; we will be happy to have you around here again. I'll give you a place to stay in one of my homes until you are able to have your own later on! Please bring everyone!"

I could not contain my joy upon hearing that news, and was already putting in my mind the thought that I will be able to make friends with Faustin's daughter Rebecca who was around my age group. Chantal and Jeanette were also happy about that, as most of our friends had been killed and it was not going to be easy to find others right away.

As we prepared to leave for Rubengera the next day, Adrie helped us put the few things we had together and we sat down and talked with her for a while before leaving. She had become a part of the family and a big sister to us. "I will miss you so much, but as soon as I get settled I will come to see you often. You all helped me to stay strong in these difficult times!" she said to us as we sat down talking. "We will come to see you also, and know that God will always be there for you, Adrie!" Mom replied.

Of course we all cried, but it wasn't the tears of sadness that we had become used to during and in the aftermath of the genocide. Chantal, Jeanette and I wished her the best and we all hugged as she walked us to the pickup truck that came to take us to Rubengera. We waved her goodbye as the truck drove away with us, bound for Rubengera.

"Do you think we will be happy living again in Rubengera with those fresh memories of the hurt and suffering we endured there?" I asked Mom as we drove. "Cherie, I understand your pain, but going back to Rubengera is our best option!" Mom replied, while Aunt Esperance nodded her head approvingly.

I personally still had a lot of trouble imagining walking around that area without Dad, and was haunted by constant thoughts of how he was tortured and killed and what had been done to me and my brothers there.

As we surveyed the hills, it became very emotional as Mom and Aunt Esperance called out the names of many friends and family we knew whose homes stood in ruins in the distance. "How are we going to be able to live seeing this daily? It's going to be really difficult for us!" echoed both Chantal and I with tears in our eyes. We were wary about people in the area and needed some time to be reassured that they had undergone a change in mindset. Those realities threatened my inner peace once more, but I quickly reversed those thoughts by reminding myself that we were about to start a new life, and it was a moment for us to be strong and live with love, not hatred for anyone despite what had happened. Thankfully we didn't have bad hearts like those who had hurt us, and I was hopeful that God would continue to be with us and help us every step of the way.

We finally arrived in Rubengera and had to prepare ourselves for whatever lay ahead. We got out of the pickup truck and walked towards Faustin's home which was near the main road. The surroundings did not present a pleasant picture and it was absolutely clear that life would not be as it was before. Nevertheless, we had to do our best to put our emotions aside and try to rebuild our lives, which we were a minute away from restarting as we approached Faustin's front door.

"Consolee, Chantal, I'm happy that you are alive and I'm glad that you will be living here!" Rebecca shouted as she and her parents ran to greet us and took us inside. "I have prepared some nicely cooked meat and vegetables with rice, and some fresh cow's milk and soda for you, with bananas for desert!" said Rachel as she and Rebecca lay the various dishes on their dining table. It was almost like a party atmosphere and a truly positive new beginning. After eating, Faustin and Rachel took us to one of their apartments and showed us a room where they told us we could stay until we are able to get our own.

"This is going to be our bedroom, living room and everything else, all in one!" said Mom, as we playfully threw ourselves on the beds. We didn't have much to put in the room as yet and five of us were able to comfortably fit in it. We considered ourselves lucky to have a place to stay, given the scarcity of accommodation in the area due to the destruction of so many homes. Faustin and his family made sure that we were comfortable and were willing to help us get whatever stuff was necessary and available. By the next day, he invited some of his friends whom he thought would be comfortable visiting us, and some came bearing small gifts!

It was a way of testing old friendships again, but it was very difficult to trust even those who didn't do anything bad or turn their backs on us during the genocide. Some of those who were mindful of our sufferings and allowed their consciences to push them came to apologize for what their people had done to all of us. We could tell that it was not easy for many of them to approach us. Their knowledge of the inhumane things that they had seen done to us may have prevented some from getting close at the beginning. For us it was difficult to approach them at first as we were still deeply heartbroken. It was going to take some time before we could feel comfortable enough to make such a move, but were able to welcome those who came to us.

"I don't hold any grudges in my heart for what was done to us, so I am able to welcome you in peace!" Mom said to a group of neighbors who had come to visit that day. "I must tell you though, that you should never make the mistake again of sitting by passively when something as cruel as genocide is being carried out against human beings like yourselves. I urge you to help bring justice to our land and teach your own kids to avoid having hatred in their hearts, and to know how wrong it was for such things to be done to other human beings!" she courageously added.

I later joked with Chantal and Jeanette and said to them: "Did you hear what Mom said to those people today? I think she definitely put the training she received in Kibingo to good use today!"

Mom showed through her interaction with those people that despite all that was done to us she didn't carry hatred, anger, or bitterness towards anyone. She inspired me so much by her courage and strength despite all the pain she had endured.

That initial period after returning to Rubengera was not pleasant to me at all and brought back difficult memories at times. As part of our new life we had to find ways to sustain ourselves, and Mom was very determined to help us as much as she could. She was the one we had to depend on and we were thankful that she had the strength and motivation to do what she was doing for us.

As we started to settle in Rubengera, Chantal, Jeanette and I were recalling a lot of the good times we had shared with our loved ones in the past. Sometimes we would be in the kitchen cooking and would start singing songs we used to sing with friends or relatives, and would suddenly find ourselves crying uncontrollably. Whenever that happened, none of us were able to stop the other from crying. Aunt Esperance knew how to return us to a good mood and was able to help us through our emotional pain. Whenever she succeeded we would start laughing and would look at each other and say: "What's wrong with us, why are we doing this?"

Our Aunt was also heartbroken herself, having went through so much, but she managed to conceal her pain while focusing on ours. She knew that we were young and needed to get back the will to live again, and most of the time she would comfort us with some nice words of hope. "God rescued us for a reason and he has a purpose for us! We need to stick to him every day and should not be afraid to ask Him for help in order to be stronger daily!" she would often say to us.

Aunt Esperance was very strong in body and spirit, but the adverse conditions under which she hid in a cramped hole for so long, affected her physically and resulted in severe pains to her back and knee. Whenever she cried out in pain I knew it was serious, as she is not someone who complains easily. Even then she would say: "Despite the fact that my body does not feel well sometimes, I am grateful to be alive and I put my whole trust in God's hands!" Aunt Esperance never made her pain visible to us, and always tried to help us bring back the joy we had known before into our lives.

We had been back in Rubengera for over a month and did not yet have the courage to go to our burnt home. It seemed like it was going to take some time for any of us to be able to go there due to the emotional pain we associated with it. Approximately two months after our return to Rubengera, however, Mom finally decided that we should visit our old home with Faustin.

Going there was very difficult for me, as the sight of the broken down structure, the thoughts about the good life we had there before, and the images of my young brothers being killed and dumped into our septic tank was simply too much to digest. Added to that, as I looked up the hill I could see the destroyed home of my paternal grandparents, and the thought that I won't see them anymore flashed through my mind! It was all very heartbreaking for me, but the worst feeling was yet to come!

As I stood there in our yard, I froze when I looked just beyond our destroyed home where Shinani had dragged me, violently beaten me with his sword and sexually assaulted me!

"Leave me alone, leave me alone or kill me right here!" I shouted, hallucinating about my past experience. I became pale and my throat suddenly dried up. "What's wrong, my child; what's wrong, Cherie?" Mom asked lovingly, with tears in her eyes.

"Sorry Mom! Can we please leave now? I lost my mind for a second and got images of the bad things that happened here and the pain inside is escalating! I'm going to scream again if I don't leave here!" We were all in tears and Faustin and Rebecca comforted us and took us back home. It was a painful evening, and as we walked home my heart was telling me that I would not be going back there anytime soon.

That night, I heard Mom walking around the room talking loudly and crying. I screamed, and we all rushed to her as none of us were fully asleep. "What happened to you Mama?" I asked as she sat down on the bed crying, and all she could say was: "My child! . . . My child! . . . . My child!" as she continued to cry for a while and slowly became calm. "I . . . I had flashbacks of seeing Bon-Fils being led away by the killers with Pascal and Philbert and I became overwhelmed with grief!" she sobbed.

It was the first time I had seen Mom display such a moment of weakness. I became worried about her and about the thoughts that were going through my own mind, and never closed my eyes for the rest of that night! It took another three months before Mom was able to go back to our old home, but for me it took more than a year.

As time went by, Chantal and I were lucky to befriend a daughter and son of the new Mayor who were about the same age as we were. They introduced us to some of their friends and we started visiting each other and developed a comfortable little self-help group able to talk and laugh together. We met regularly at the mayor's residence and he encouraged us to stay over and have small parties at times to create some fun and learn to smile again.

Those moments of "letting go" made me feel that life was coming back slowly, and I started to adjust and was able to think that in spite of all that I went through, God would help me move on from there and have a life I deserve. It was good therapy for all of us but no one knew then that we had become our own 'therapists!'

As people in the neighborhood started getting more comfortable with us being back in Rubengera, they were bringing information to us about the killers of some of our relatives. We were at home one day when an old neighbor named Jason came home to see Mom and appeared very excited to speak with her.

"I have seen Damas, the person who had killed Ngoga! He is back in the village acting as if he never did anything wrong! I personally saw Damas chase Ngoga and after catching up with him, he took off the shirt and shoes he was wearing, and tortured and killed him! He even had the gall to wear Ngoga's shirt and shoes as a show of pride!" Jason disdainfully told Mom.

Mom became sad but was glad for the information and immediately reported Damas to the RPF authority who took him to prison. When the authorities first questioned him he denied having killed my dad. We later confronted him at the prison and it was evident that he was going through hell within himself. By the way he looked, I am sure that what he had done to my dad and others may have already been haunting him. I was really hurt within my heart but felt that if he won't admit and apologize from the heart, the guilt would keep destroying him, so I left it up to God.

Some weeks later we were pleasantly surprised when one of my mom's cousins showed up at our new home one Sunday. "Sister Agnes is here! Sister Agnes is here!" Jeanette shouted as Mom peeked outside to look. "You're most welcome Sister Agnes. We are so happy to see you alive!" said Mom as she met her at the door. As she sat down and made herself comfortable, Sister Agnes related to us about her ordeals in Cyangugu Prefecture during the genocide. We were all happy to see her and to know that she had survived. She spent about a week with us, and during that time we talked a lot. I told her some of the hurtful things that had happened to me, and she comforted me through positive words and spiritual teachings, which helped me a lot. I hoped she would stay with us longer but she apologized and told us that she had to go.

"Do not be angry with those who are responsible! You must pray always to gain the power to forgive them and be able to move on with your lives!" she urged all of us before she left.

More than a year after that visit Sister Agnes informed us by letter that she would be coming for another vacation with us, but unfortunately she became victim to an ambush by Interahamwe infiltrators while on her way to Kibuye. The bus she was traveling in was attacked and riddled with bullets which killed a number of occupants and wounded others. She was among the wounded, shot in the chest and leg, but was later taken to Belgium for treatment and survived her injuries.

Despite whatever circumstances she faced, Sister Agnes always wore a genuine smile and carried no anger in her heart towards those who hurt her. She lives day by day working to make people smile wherever she is and showing love to whoever is around her. She is one of my favorite aunts and her goodness towards others taught us to become better people in our own lives. Although I did not get to meet her very often, whenever we met she always lifted my spirit and made me feel strong. Her favorite words to me were **"Life must go on! Be strong and never give up, because God loves you!"** I often think of her and ask God to let me be like her because she inspires me.

★ ★ ★

REFLECTIONS ON CHAPTER 14

We as human beings have the power and knowledge to know what's wrong and what's right and the will to choose between them. We are the most intelligent among God's created species, with the ability and capacity to do many things which no other species on earth can. God is always speaking to us and telling us how he wants us to be every day.

I believe that each person has the capacity within themselves to feel good when they genuinely do something nice to someone else. Likewise, when people commit evil acts against others, they also have the capacity to feel bad within themselves for what they have done. Goodness or evil within people have a tendency to also show on the outside through their behavior, demeanor and actions towards others. Knowing that all our behaviors start from the inside and later manifest on the outside, we should always try to control what's going through our minds and try to convert the negative thoughts into positive ones.

Sometimes people are motivated to hurt others for the sole purpose of gaining material things or to satisfy egotistical tendencies, but truly they are also hurting themselves without realizing it. I believe that if each and every one of us become more tolerant and show more goodwill towards one another despite our differences, and prevent hatred from overtaking our minds, our world will be a better place for all of us to co-exist in genuine peace and harmony.

As I write on this issue I am compelled to reflect on the efforts of Mother Teresa whom I admired so much for what she has done during her remarkable lifetime to foster that deep sense of love for every human being, especially the poor, sick and downtrodden. She was very inspiring to the world and some of the things she has said and done continue to touch me deeply. If we can all follow her example, our love for each other will spread and will ultimately replace hatred wherever it shows its ugly head in the world.

CHAPTER 15

FACING NEW CHALLENGES

One day Faustin's neighbor Etienne, came to our house with Calvin, his former neighbor who had moved to the capital Kigali after the genocide. They sat down with Mom and told her that they had something to tell her. Mom was "all ears" as she sat back in her chair, eager to hear what they had to say.

"Miss Jeanne, my friend here has found this guy Shinani who used to be your neighbor! He killed many people in the area during the genocide including my brother in law!" Etienne said excitedly. "I'm not surprised. He also attacked us during the genocide and I have heard many other stories about him!" Mom replied.

"You know, I was in Cyangugu recently and I saw him selling stuff in one of the markets. I couldn't stand seeing that killer walking around so freely, knowing that he had killed so many people, so the minute I saw him I went to the authorities and reported him!" Calvin chimed in. "They put him in prison and told me that I need to bring witnesses to support my claim within three days. I want this killer to pay for what he has done, and I knew he had also done bad things to your family, so I came for your help!" Calvin added eagerly.

"We will help you! That man-killer has hurt my beloved child and raped her and I want him to face trial and never be let out again!" Mom replied, with tears streaming down her face.

"Fantastic! Can you talk it over with your daughter and confirm that she is willing to go with us to Cyangugu to report what had happened to her?" Etienne responded enthusiastically.

Calvin and Etienne left shortly after, promising to return later. After they left, Mom sat me down and I could see that her eyes were welling up with tears. "Mom, you look unhappy; are you okay?" I asked enquiringly. "My child, as you see I was talking to Etienne and his friend and they told me that they saw the horrible person who hurt you! I want you to go and testify to the authorities in Cyangugu about what he did to you!"

It took a moment for the information to sink in, while Mom quickly added: "I know how difficult it is, but I need you to try to go my dear child and explain what he did, in whatever way you can."

As I began to process what she had just told me, the reality of what I had to do hit me like a ton of bricks! I started crying uncontrollably, unable to speak and she held me in her arms, still crying herself. I was in deep emotional pain, and she comforted me until I managed to pull myself together and felt that I was able to speak again.

"Mom I will go and try!" I said bravely as I wiped away the last speck of tears from my swollen eyes. "My child, I pray that God will be with you!" she promptly replied with a smile. I had made up my mind that I could not tolerate seeing Shinani walking around freely without being punished for what he had done to me and others. The next day, still deeply pained and unsure of how I was going to face that horrible man, I went with Etienne and Calvin to the prison in Cyangugu. As we arrived, an officer came out and spoke with me.

"I know what you have been through, my dear, but you will not have to go through such abuse any longer. I'd like you to relax and tell me what happened!" he said in a calm and reassuring tone. Although he was really nice and was careful about the way he spoke to me, the images were haunting me and I started shaking as though it was happening there and then! I couldn't speak, and was crying uncontrollably. Etienne, Calvin and the officer calmed me down while another officer brought Shinani out to where I was.

As soon as Shinani saw me he started yelling like an evil and crazed person, probably trying to intimidate me, but the officer immediately shut him up. Seeing him so close was very frightening, as what he had done to me was still fresh in my mind. Still shaking, I was finally able to tell the officer the details of what Shinani had done to me on that fateful night in May.

When I was finished the officer looked at me sadly, held my hand and said: "Don't worry, you'll be fine, and he will pay for what he did to you!" His words were very encouraging but I needed to leave that place! I didn't want to keep facing that terrible man any more than I had to! The wound in my heart was deep and it was going to take a while to heal, but again I was still very young and I prayed within that I would get to the point where I would become stronger and be able to move beyond that terrible chapter of my life.

By mid to late 1995 the new administration was doing everything it could to help students return to school and bring other social structures in the country back to normal. As one can imagine, the genocide experience made it difficult for many of us affected kids to go back to the classrooms and be able to focus. There were so many orphans who were deeply traumatized and had no means of receiving professional therapy, and thus couldn't readjust easily to studying as they used to. Many were left alone without an immediate family member to talk to and support them in their struggles. In essence, the genocide had taken away what a child needs most to help them grow up in a natural way . . . that is, parental care and guidance.

Around October of that year, schools throughout the country had resumed operations and Mom was one of the teachers recalled to her teaching job at the Rubengera Elementary School. We thought it would be difficult for her to teach those kids in the area, some of whose relatives were responsible for killing her young kids, husband and parents, while others had participated in alerting killers about where we were hiding. As she prepared herself for her first day back at school, I was curious to know how she felt about going back. "Mom, how will you be able to teach those kids, some of whose parents and relatives were responsible for killing Dad and our brothers?" I asked in earnest. "Well my child, it is simple! I am determined to do my job with the same confidence, willingness and good heart just as I used to before. I am not prepared to carry the burden of those misguided people on my shoulders and I cannot allow the kids to suffer for what their parents and relatives did!" she courageously replied.

Mom had obviously made a choice to remain good at heart despite everything, and that was her way of living true to her character, knowing that doing bad to others was not the answer for the bad things others had done to her. I was touched by her extraordinary courage and spirit, but being a young traumatized kid I was not yet able to operate at her level.

As fate would have it, upon Mom's resumption of teaching at the Rubengera Elementary School, Sanani's sister Christine was also assigned as a teacher there, and their classrooms were situated next to each other. Over time, Christine's actions towards her gave Mom an indication that she was genuinely bothered by what her brother had done to our family. Christine slowly started communicating with her, and openly expressed regrets for what Sanani had done to my brothers. As Mom told me later, she responded by showing Christine that she held no hatred or anger towards her or her family and accepted her as a friend once again.

I felt that for me it would be difficult going back to school in Rubengera and I wondered if I was able to operate as Mom was able to do with Christine so soon after the genocide. Mom was very understanding of the fragile state I was in, and decided to enroll me in the Apade Secondary School in the capital Kigali far away from home. I readily agreed and reminded myself of what I used to tell Dad when he was alive about wanting to be educated and able to achieve my goals in life. Despite my pain, I truly wanted to do my best to keep that promise.

In my first few days at Apade I tried to introduce myself to others, but wasn't able to connect as well as I wanted. Most of the other students knew each other, as they lived in the city and had known one another before. I was constantly having thoughts of what had happened to me, and I didn't feel like I was on the same level as they were. The first trimester at school was a nightmare. I was alone with no friends and it was becoming worse within me day by day. The psychological wounds were still open and I couldn't focus on what I was doing in school. Day after day things were going badly for me and it was not getting better in the way I hoped it would.

I used to have constant thoughts and images of the horrors we had faced during those tragic three months, but I kept trying to be strong. In contrast, sometimes when I was not dwelling on those bad images, I would recall all the good times I spent with Dad and the good teachings and affection he had given us at home. In those moments of thought I would also imagine how great it would have been to know that he would be there on my wedding day if and when that time ever comes, to hold my hand and walk me down the aisle and give me his blessings.

Whenever these good and bad memories came, it felt like I was rewinding and fast forwarding two different movies in my head at the same time. It constantly broke my heart to know that he is gone and all that he prepared for us was also gone. Those were very difficult moments for me because I loved my dad so much and I felt cheated by being forced to live day by day without him around.

My second trimester at Apade was fast approaching, and I sat in my friend's living room the Sunday before the restart of classes, dreading how I was going to cope. The next day while at school I heard someone call my name as I was walking to my classroom. As I turned around, to my surprise I saw it was a friend from Rubengera named Laetitia.

"Consolee, I have good news!" she said jubilantly. "Oh my goodness, Laetitia . . . It's so good to see you here! What's the good news?" I asked eagerly. "I'll be attending Apade starting today!" Laetitia gleefully replied. "Are you for real?" I asked delightedly. "That's fantastic news! You don't know how much you have made my day, girl!" I added.

Laetitia is a survivor who I had gotten to know in Rubengera after the genocide, and she was placed in the same class as me that day. It was a relief for me and I felt a little better as she was psychologically stronger than I was and I felt that she could help me to get through my turbulence. She did not take long to adjust, and soon enough she got close to some students who also became friends with me. Laetitia managed to get through her classes pretty well and I was thankful that she was not as badly affected as I was.

Even with Laetitia there as support, I still wasn't able to focus in the classroom. I was not feeling well within myself and my mind was constantly elsewhere, dwelling on my past experiences. No matter how I tried to push them out of my mind, it was no use. I felt horrible and had to keep fighting within, but those haunting thoughts were affecting me to the point that I was no longer able to converse with my classmates.

As the trimester progressed, some of them kept looking at me with curiosity until one student couldn't hold it any longer. "Consolee, are you okay? You always seem to be so distant!" she asked me one day. "I'm okay, thanks for asking!" I replied, wishing to make the conversation as brief as possible. She glanced at me with a puzzled look on her face and walked away shaking her head.

Many of them were too young to see directly through my hurt, but were able to observe that I was withdrawn and not making any progress in the classroom, as I failed every test we had in every subject! Laetitia became very concerned and told me one day: "Consolee, I don't want you to keep getting these grades, failing all the time; let's work together after school and maybe that will help!"

"Yes, it would be nice and I'm willing to do it!" I replied spontaneously, just to please her. I had very little control over the psychological turmoil that was taking place within me and I wasn't yet ready to tell her how I truly felt. I didn't know how to say it, and didn't know if it would be the best way to help myself.

A few months later I started getting ill frequently, was easily irritated, and felt less energetic in my body. This made me fearful that my psychological issues were also affecting my physical health, but I tried to hide all those feelings to avoid any criticism from those around. As young as Laetitia herself was, she managed to help me without knowing exactly what was really bothering me. It was in her own understanding to help her friend who was having difficulties, without judging my performances in class.

"You don't need to be alone during the weekend, Consolee! Why don't you join me to visit some of my family friends?" Laetitia would offer when Friday evening came around. That helped me a lot as there was nothing pleasing to me in those times.

Having Laetitia around made me feel a little better, but my psychological trauma wasn't going anywhere. At the end of each trimester I did poorly and I felt bad about it, as I wasn't like that when Dad was around. None of the teachers took note that I was having a problem, or asked why I was not doing well in the classroom. I guess they may have thought I was failing because I was not serious about school or was distracting myself by other things.

At the end of the year I left to go home for vacation, and on the way I started thinking about what I needed to do in order to feel and perform better in school. I thought about switching to a school near home where I would be able to control things better with the support of my family around me. That seemed to be my best option and I was ready to tell Mom about my situation and make a decision that would be best for me!

After arriving back home in Rubengera I felt like a huge load had been taken off my head. I was laughing and giggling with everyone at home, and was able to sleep without those haunting thoughts bothering me. A week later I was ready to sit down to talk with my mom!

"Mom, I'm not going back to that school in Kigali! I said to her that day at breakfast. "What's the matter Cherie? Did you have problems there?" she asked, as a worried frown creased her face. "I feel that I should study near here because of my health conditions. In the future I won't mind, but right now I am not ready to be so far away from you all!" I said to her. Mom looked at me and I could immediately see that as a parent she understood the difficulties I had.

"Don't worry, Cherie, we will arrange for you to go to a school nearby. I don't want you to feel uncomfortable and become sick; I want you to be able to study well and succeed in the classroom!" she said to me.

Mom was the only person I was able to tell whatever I truly felt within me during those fragile periods of my life. Dwelling on that reality, I thought about all those orphaned kids who had been through similar experiences and how hard it must be for them every single day, living without loved ones to provide such comfort to them and understand their innermost pains and difficulties. Since my return home from Kigali, both my psychological and physical outlook had improved. I smiled more often and had fun with friends and started to slowly regain my confidence. I realized that being at home close to my mom, aunt, cousin, and my young sister was a good form of healing for me which I could not get anywhere else.

"Oh, I'm so happy that I'll be attending school right next door!" I said to Mom, as I headed towards the Rubengera High School that Monday morning. "I'm so eager to start there and I know I will do better than I did at Apade!" I added, overflowing with confidence. Mom was also happy for me and kept smiling as she stood there looking at me as I disappeared in the distance.

As time went on, there were moments when I couldn't dismiss the fear that I might be infected as a result of the sexual assault I had endured during the genocide. I tried to ignore it but kept dwelling on the thought of what life would be like for me if I was. Given the severe stigma associated with HIV at that time, I feared that if I got really sick, my physical makeup would deteriorate rapidly and people would start avoiding me as though I had the plague. Sometimes the fear would become so intense that I would speak indirectly about it with Mom who would always offer comforting words to me and make me feel better. She would often tell me: "My child be strong, let us keep on praying everyday without ceasing so that God will keep surrounding you with his protection. He rescued you for a purpose and will be with you throughout; keep him first in your heart!"

Mom helped me through those fears and my focus on schoolwork was getting better. I was also getting myself involved in other activities which I felt would help me in school and increase my energy and love of life. I started participating in traditional dance classes after school, and that brought me closer to my classmates and boosted my energy level, and I was able to better control the things that hurt me in the past. It was a long tough journey to get there but I remained strong and fought hard every single day and was praying non stop in order to succeed.

Whenever I discovered something that helped me feel great, I stuck to it because I needed to utilize every strategy that worked for me. I was thankful for every one of them, as there were no professional therapists to help me out, and there was little or no likelihood that such type of "luxury medical treatment" would be made available to anyone anytime soon. I had to try on my own to overcome what had destroyed my innocence and part of my childhood.

★ ★ ★

REFLECTIONS ON CHAPTER 15

When a person has experienced the levels and multiplicity of physical and emotional traumas that survivors had to deal with, it could never be easy for them to go back to a normal way of life, especially if professional counseling is not available to them. You feel like your world has come crashing down on you and you are unable to pick up the pieces.

After the genocide, my ability to focus was almost zero due to the many conflicts that were going through my mind and body, and the results were evident in the poor grades that I started to obtain for the first time in my school career. Even today I still have problems in maintaining my focus and this poses a challenge for me at times.

Although my near death experiences and the pains I have suffered during the genocide have forced me to look at life in general from a different perspective, I have made a conscious decision to continue living the way Mom and Dad taught me to live—with love and compassion for others.

CHAPTER 16

STRUGGLING WITH EMOTIONS

Talking to some orphaned kids one day, it broke my heart to hear how one 9 year old girl described her situation. "It's so difficult to live with such heavy issues that are constantly in my mind. It makes me feel like the world is on top of my head and I don't know how to live in a normal way, as everything I do is such a challenge!" she said to me in a sad tone.

This was about two years after the genocide, and like that 9 year old girl, most, if not all other survivors were having tough times trying to live day by day. Many had lost the sense of what life meant to them. In addition to the psychological trauma which we had suffered, a large percentage had also experienced varying types of physical trauma that left them with visible scars, serving as a grim reminder to them every single day.

For hundreds of thousands of young kids left orphaned and forced to become heads of households like that poor little girl, it was doubly worse. Some of them had lived through the indignity of seeing their mothers or sisters raped in front of them and in some cases later killed—such a terrible thing for anyone to experience. I actually have a friend who was around my age at the time, whose mother was raped in his presence and later killed by her attackers. Added to that, every one of his close relatives were also killed so he had to find ways and means to provide for himself after the genocide.

With their parents and close family members gone, one can just imagine the difficulties these kids faced having to provide for their younger siblings without a proper place to live, no possessions or income, and having to deal with their own trauma and that of their younger brothers and sisters. On one of the occasions that I spoke to them, another brave kid told me something which highlighted their plight, but which also touched me deeply.

"As kids we are supposed to have parents to take care of us, but the cruel genocide has left us with the impossible task of caring for ourselves and our siblings!" he said, with a feeling of hopelessness. His words which were uttered with such emotion, still resonate in my mind even today, and has been a constant source of worry for me.

I also recall the plight of Jill, a fellow survivor and friend, who had a very difficult time after the genocide. Like me, she had tried going back to school but couldn't focus on her schoolwork. One day we were speaking about our experiences and I was curious to know whether her lack of focus could be attributed to reasons that were similar to mine, so I asked her about it.

I was not surprised in the least when she told me in response: "The physical scars I had from being severely chopped in my back left me disfigured and physically challenged, and the pain of seeing the scars and the constant physical difficulties I had was a daily reminder of what I had been through. It was very difficult for me, as I couldn't control the bad memories which constantly flooded my brain whenever I was in class!"

I was able to easily relate to what Jill had been through, and I tried my best to console her by telling her she was not alone in that situation. "Don't worry my dear, the psychological difficulties you experienced in class were very similar to what I faced! I know you tried your best to cope but many people will not understand what you were going through!" I said, empathizing with her.

Jill eventually dropped out of school and created her own clothing business which she was able to put her heart into and began doing very well. Seeing my fellow survivor and friend succeed everyday with those large scars and reduced mobility, gave me loads of encouragement and I truly admired her strength!

There were many others who didn't have the strength to overcome their pain and to do anything for themselves or their loved ones, as their situation had become too overwhelming for them. I saw many widows and orphans in my home area who struggled to live day by day, and some of them appeared to have lost the will to live. Some of the widows living in the area visited Mom regularly to relate their stresses to her, and she would freely give of her time to talk to them. I was very touched by what a widow told Mom one day when she stopped by to talk.

"Miss Jeanne, one of the most pressing needs that many of us have is for someone to listen to us about the different things we went through and to feel that others understand our plight. If we can restore our will to live, we would become motivated to do what we can to satisfy those other needs. Many of us have already given up and feel that life is not worth living!" she said sadly.

Mom dedicated her free time to help those widows deal with their trauma. She also had to provide that constant ear for Jeanette, Chantal and I. Knowing that we were still growing and the pain had affected us in different ways, she needed to pay close attention and provide the special care we needed for us to function well every day. Fortunately for us, Aunt Esperance was there to help her with those challenges! Mom and Aunt Esperance were the only parents we had left, so they had to become stronger for us, and thankfully they were always there to share our pains.

Mom and Aunt Esperance were trying hard not to show the pain they carried from the genocide, but as strong as they appeared, the toll it had taken on them was showing in varying 'forms and fashions.' There are things that each of them was doing which were totally uncharacteristic, but I knew it was the effect of the genocide. I sometimes thought that they were not affected because of the way they were helping us on a daily basis, but they were simply trying their best to be strong in order to be there for us. Whenever they looked at us it was clear that they wanted us to rise above our emotional pain, but they themselves were deeply broken and it was a constant fight within them.

Prior to the genocide Mom was never a person who would go to bed before us. After work she would normally find things to do around the house like tending to her garden, making sure that we all ate, did our homework, and went to bed on time. After the genocide when she resumed her teaching job at school, I started to observe that she would come home from work around 5pm, take a shower and go straight to her bedroom and would not come out until the next morning, not even to have dinner. I became concerned about her and decided to speak to Aunt Esperance about it one day.

"Aunty, I'm worried about Mom. She does not stick around to be with us when she comes home from work like she used to. Do you think she is lonely or suffering from depression?" I asked. "Macwa, I have observed that myself, and am also wondering what could be the problem! Don't worry; she may just be tired after working hard every day. I will talk with her tomorrow and try to find out if she has a problem!" Aunt Esperance replied.

The next evening, Aunt Esperance followed Mom into her room and stayed with her for about an hour while I waited outside with Chantal and Jeanette. "What did she tell you Aunty?" I whispered in her ear as she closed the door after exiting Mom's room. "Children, you need not worry; your Mom has been through a lot and just needs some time alone to relax her mind," she said to us. "Well, we understand, but can't she spend at least an hour with us before she goes to relax?" I enquired.

It seemed like Aunt Esperance knew more than she was telling us and was weighing the information to make sure she doesn't say something that would make us feel bad. Creases formed on her forehead as she shook her head and said: "Your mom is okay, but she is very traumatized by the loss of your father and her three babies and the difficulties she had been through. We need to give her some time to recover, as she does not feel like doing anything and only gets some peace when she meditates in her room!"

I listened to what my aunt had to say, but decided that I needed to check up on Mom every single day. I felt that she was alone and somehow it was neither helping us nor her, and I myself needed to have a constant conversation with her in order to ease my internal pain.

The very next evening, I went to see Mom in her bedroom and tried to convince her to come 'hang out' with us before we go to bed, to avoid bringing back bad memories to her mind. "No, my child, I'm sorry. I'm okay with my thoughts but I just don't feel in the mood to talk or do anything, as I don't have the energy," she replied in answer to my pleadings.

It was clear that she was not buying into my argument, so I instead hatched a plan and brought a chair which I placed in her bedroom and left. The next evening I bolted into her room bubbling with excitement and found her lying quietly on the bed. "Hi Mom, I have something to tell you today!" I said to her with a broad smile. "What is it, my child?" she asked weakly. "I have some jokes to tell you that will surely make you laugh, Mom!" I replied.

From that evening, I made it my duty to go there and sit with her and tell her funny jokes which we would both laugh at, and also talk about positive issues with her in order to lift her spirit. I started realizing that she enjoyed what I was saying and laughed heartily whenever I said something funny. I did not give her jokes and fun talk every day though, as there were times I would bring to her some issues that were hurtful to me, knowing that she is a good listener and that I could discuss with her anything I felt like talking about. I wished I didn't have to bother Mom with things that were hurting me, but the genocide had broken me in so many ways and those memories of what happened were still coming through my head. I really needed to talk to her about them in order to feel better within!

As Mom started to improve her mood, mine appeared to have started to decline. I wasn't sleeping quite well and used to get nightmares of all the terrible things that had happened to us, and sometimes I would get up and sit on the bed trembling, thinking the events were just happening, and would start crying. Those nightmares were coming very often and I couldn't control them, and whenever I had them I couldn't breathe sometimes.

I tried different coping mechanisms such as listening to music to soothe my mind whenever I was alone, or going to meet with Sister Louise our mentor and friend from the nearby convent, who was a great adviser to us. I also prayed a lot, and would say in my prayers everyday: "God, please help me get back to normal and help me face life without being bothered by those painful memories." I was trying anything to overcome the nagging thoughts that were coming through my brain.

I wanted so badly to go back to how it was before when I had both parents around and felt the goodness every day of them loving me and allowing me to grow and dream about the best things for my life.

I believe the different coping mechanisms I tried worked in some way, for as time went by, I found myself slowly feeling more in control of my thoughts and was able to sleep longer with less mental disturbances. My trust in God never stopped because I continued to believe in him for any situation in my life. I became closer to Him and I wanted Him to live within me throughout. As young as I was, I couldn't help but feel sometimes that life was over for me and I could never be able to accomplish any of my goals. Despite that feeling, I still had a strong will to live, so I fought hard within myself so that I could be able to dream again and restore the feeling that I could be productive to myself and my community in the future.

After months of isolating herself in her bedroom after work, Mom finally got her motivation back and reverted to spending much of her evening talking with us. We spoke about any and everything we felt like discussing, and it was evident that every one of us had changed in some ways. Jeanette had also gone through so many changes and started to also get nightmares and would often awaken from sleep screaming. She also had difficulty focusing in school and started blaming herself, which worsened it. Knowing her pain, I tried to encourage her as an older sister but it wasn't helping much. She was a troubled child who needed professional help which was not available to her. Despite her issues, I thanked God each day for rescuing her. She is my baby sister whom I love so much and always will till the day I die.

Chantal has been through so much herself but the way she coped was amazing. She is naturally very sociable in character and that helped her a lot in dealing with her stresses, even though she too had moments when the memories of her experiences would emotionally overwhelm her. She remains unfazed and is so mentally strong that even today no one could tell without knowing what she has been through, that she is a survivor of such a dreadful genocide. She became a great "sister" to me and we helped each other through our difficult teenage years despite all that we carried within us. I thank God she survived and I love her so much.

Months later, I started to feel more in control of my thoughts, and during one of our evening discussions with Mom, I decided to raise a burning issue which I felt was disturbing each and every one of us in the house. "Mom, I think it's time that we go to our burnt out home and visit Philbert, Pascal and Bon-Fils whose bodies are lying in our septic tank!" I said, to Mom's utter surprise. The faces of everyone at the table dropped as they all became silent, with tears welling up in their eyes. "I miss them every day and want to communicate with them and I feel it's time that we give them a decent burial Mom!" I added sadly, with tears also streaming down my face.

Our septic tank was fairly deep and it would take some effort and discomfort to get them, but I felt we had to do it. Mom was still very heartbroken thinking about the horror of them being killed and thrown in the tank, and admitted to us that she wasn't yet able to handle the pain of seeing their skeletons. "Children, please bear with me, as you know I recently helped bury your aunt Rose and two of your dear cousins, and almost lost my sanity on seeing their remains!" Mom pleaded.

The scars were too deep and she needed time to recompose herself before she could take on the heavy burden of burying my brothers. The time she needed, however, was longer than I imagined and I ended up leaving Rwanda before she got the courage to do it. It took her fifteen years before she was finally able to retrieve their skeletons from the septic tank, having done so on May 2, 2009, when they were buried at a memorial site in Kibuye. I miss them and my dad more than anyone else in the world but I know they are in a good place.

Many people in the country had committed genocide crimes, and the jails were severely overcrowded. The court system was unable to cope with the multitude of cases that had to be tried, so the government had to find another way to bring those accused to justice. They created a system called GACACA, which in earlier times was a traditional way to reconcile conflicts between families and neighbors.

Respected members of the community were trained to serve in the panels of judges throughout the country, and local residents would give testimony for and against the suspects in their communities where the genocidal crimes were committed. It turned out to be a very good way to know who the killers were and to get accused persons to confess. Under the system, those against whom there was evidence and who refused to acknowledge their crimes would be punished accordingly if found guilty, but those who confessed in GACACA courts would have their sentences reduced, or would in some cases be freed if they had already served enough time in prison.

This system caused a lot of anxiety for survivors at the beginning, as many of the killers refused to admit what they had done even though most of the acts had been committed in plain view of many people. Some were able to apologize to their victims or their families but it was very difficult for survivors to face those that were in denial, especially when victims knew in their hearts what the perpetrators had done to them or their families, and were blatantly denying it in their presence.

I was not able to participate in GACACA because I migrated to the USA just about the time when their hearings started. Some years later, I called my Mom one day for our usual chit chat on the phone. As she picked up the phone I could immediately sense some tension in her voice. "Ma Cherie, you would not believe what I received yesterday!" Filled with curiosity, I quickly said to her: "Tell me, tell me, what is it?" With pain in her voice, she said to me: "I received a letter from Sanani, the neighbor who had killed your brothers. He is in prison and has asked me for forgiveness!"

I was a bit confused by the news, and she said: "Don't worry, let me read to you his complete letter and you would understand better!" I sobbed as Mom read out to me the hand-written letter, a copy of which is included in this book. When translated into English, it reads:

"To Mrs. Marie Jeanne Mukamwiza, I am writing to ask for your forgiveness from the bottom of my heart because I have done wrong killing your children. Truly, throughout the years our families lived together harmoniously; when I needed some money or in my daily struggles, your husband had always been there for me and helped me. I beg you to forgive me, I admit the wrongdoing I have committed knowing

that there was no problem between us. May God forgive me and may
all of you, whom I have hurt, also forgive me.

Thank you. Signed: Sanani.

After reading his apology Mom could only cry and told me that she did not immediately respond to him, but about two weeks later he was taken to face trial at the GACACA court. Mom and Aunt Esperance went there to hear what he was going to say and to assess whether he was sincere.

As Sanani started to speak to the court, he knelt down in front of my mom crying incessantly and said: *"I'm so sorry to God and to you Jeanne and to everyone for what I did. I was horrible and I feel disgusted within myself for my wrongdoings. These kids whose lives I took, were great kids and they were going to be good to me as you and your family always were. I didn't gain anything except guilt in my heart. I'm so sorry Jeanne!"*

Mom told me that she was overcome by Sanani's apparent remorse and looked at him with pity and said to him "I forgive you, but I hope you know that true forgiveness is ultimately up to God's judgment!" She later told me that she truly forgave him because it was best for her and she felt he was genuinely remorseful for what he had done.

I was happy that at least my brothers' killer had apologized for the heinous act he had committed against them, but I kept struggling with the thought that so many others were refusing to apologize. I thought about Shinani who had sexually terrorized me, and of others who had betrayed our right to coexist and killed our loved ones and friends. It was a constant struggle in my thoughts which I kept asking God in my daily prayers to help me deal with. I later found a great deal of peace within myself after I decided to put them all into God's hands and asked him to keep helping me avoid having any bad thoughts about them.

It's a difficult journey to get to the point where you can forgive after so many viciously unjust things have been done to you, but through God's grace I believe I have reached that point. I am truly convinced that there could be no peace in the hearts of those killers when they remember all the innocent blood they have shed, and such consolation has helped me to move on and live my life without anger or hatred towards anyone. It doesn't mean that whoever committed those horrible acts should not face justice. I believe that while forgiveness frees the hearts and minds of victims from carrying the burdens that their aggressors should instead be carrying, justice is still very important, especially for those who are unrepentant for the wrong they have done to others. Through the GACACA system and other methods employed by the government, some have learned that the ideology of hatred and ethnic extermination is bad and hopefully will never be repeated in Rwanda or anywhere else.

★   ★   ★

REFLECTIONS ON CHAPTER 16

Whenever I pray, I ask God to keep being with all of my fellow survivors because they are really heartbroken and need healing from all their wounds. They suffered terribly and there are so many long term consequences which they have to deal with as a result of the genocide. A few of the more apparent ones are as follows:

There are so many women who were brutally and repeatedly raped and impregnated or infected with HIV, resulting in a multiplicity of physical, emotional and social trauma. They are deeply hurt and have limited resources to deal with their pain.

Not every survivor has been able to know the circumstances of their loved ones' death or find their remains to give them a decent burial, so there will never be closure for many of them.

Survivors will carry the trauma of the genocide throughout their lives, and are in need of more support and counseling.

Genocide is one of the worst things that human kind can do to their fellow men, and the Rwanda experience in 1994 ranks among the worst in history due to the excessively large number of lives that were taken in such a short period of time. We have seen it happen to vulnerable groups across the globe from century to century and yet we have not learned that this blatant disregard for human life does not belong in civil society.

Yesterday it was Rwanda, today it could be somewhere else, that's why we need the help of each and every one to fight against any type of violence against humanity that is occurring anywhere.

CHAPTER 17

TESTING FOR HIV

During the genocide, rape was used as a weapon against women with the intent of infecting them with HIV. Many of them were gang raped and suffered the misfortune of being impregnated in the process. There were also those who didn't get pregnant but contracted HIV and worse yet, others who got pregnant *and* contracted HIV as well.

Apart from having to deal with the emotional trauma directly associated with the acts, many of those women in Rwanda were forced to become mothers to infants whose fathers were unknown for the most part and were part of groups responsible for torturing the victims. Some of them also had to deal with the additional trauma of discovering their HIV positive status and living un-medicated with the virus in the aftermath of the genocide, when even the most basic health care was not available.

As a young girl who was raped, I struggled with so many things within me. I was devastated internally and had to pray constantly to God to prevent me from thinking about it. I remember during the first months following the attack I became very weak compared to my sister and mother who were living under the same conditions as me, and my first thought then was: "What if I have contracted HIV from that terrible man?"

I always tried to push that thought away from my mind as I could not bear to imagine how I would handle being HIV positive. I was terribly scared but hopeful, and kept monitoring my body all the time, fearing to go for testing. I didn't want to know because I thought I would die the minute it was confirmed.

About four years after the attack on me, I remember getting up one morning and I observed some unusual little bumps showing up on my legs. I became stressed about them but tried not to show it. The bumps would become red and itchy and would dry up and heal on their own after a few days. I became concerned and felt that I had to tell Mom.

"Mom, I have been seeing these weird bumps on my legs for the past weeks and I'm getting worried about them!" I said to Mom, as I raised my skirt to show her. "Don't worry, Cherie, I don't think it's anything serious. I'm sure they'll eventually go away!" she replied, while looking at the bumps. I was hoping she would say something like that and was relieved when she said it, but deep down I still felt perturbed about them.

Those bumps never went away for good, and during my last year of high school they kept showing up and disappearing. I was doing all I could to prevent my mind from thinking that I might be infected, and tried to overcome the common cold or other ailments quickly, thinking that if I looked sick, I was going to be rejected by the society. For that reason, I did not speak to anyone about my fears.

By the time I finished high school, I was happy but was still concerned about those bumps on my legs, and spent a lot of time praying for the fear of having HIV to go away. I frequently spoke directly to God, saying: "God, I know you made me survive the genocide because you have a purpose for my life! Please help me get the fear of HIV from my mind!"

Sometimes after praying I would feel confident that I was fine, but the fear always came back. As much as I was praying to God to help me, he was planning other ways by which he wanted me to know whether I was sick or not. I didn't want to go to the doctor to find out, but it appears as though He had other plans for me. My cousin had migrated to the USA with her husband about a year before I finished high school and I kept in contact with them through phone calls and letters.

One day in 2001 my cousin and her husband called me from New York. "Consolee, how are you?" she asked briefly. "Oh, I'm fine, thanks!" I replied.

"Me and my husband were talking and thought about asking you to come and join us in New York. What do you think?" Before she could finish, I screamed with joy and said "Yes, Yes! When can I come, tomorrow?" I asked, overcome with joy.

"Hey, I know you are happy, but take it easy! You need to have a passport and visa to travel, you know!" she replied.

I couldn't wait to tell Mom the news and ran to meet her as she walked up to the house after work that evening. "Mom, I am going to America!" I told her, smiling from ear to ear. "You're what? What are you talking about, Macwa? I hope you are not hallucinating again!" she said curiously. "No Mom, Immaculee and her husband called today and told me they will arrange for me to come and join them! Aren't you happy for me?" I replied.

Mom's face lighted up when she realized I was serious and, smiling broadly, took me inside and said. "Okay, we have to plan. I will call New York tomorrow and speak to them. I'm so happy for you, my child!"

I was so happy and wished all the arrangements could be made that day so I can travel the next day. I was pleased at the possibility of changing my environment to one where I could be sheltered from any negativity if it turned out that I was HIV positive. I was also very excited about the prospect, knowing that in a place like America I could get professional counseling that could heal my troubling feelings and fears.

Chantal, my other cousin who was like a sister to me, was already there and I was looking forward to joining her. I arrived in the USA not long after and felt better prepared to face up to what was going on in my body, away from my home environment. After I arrived, despite feeling that my fear of HIV had lessened, I was still afraid of going to get tested, and was not prepared to tell anyone about the bumps on my legs.

After about a year in New York those troubling bumps started to multiply all over my legs and I became really scared. I was also having fever, headaches and sometimes unusual fatigue, but I was afraid to face the possibility that I might truly be infected with HIV. I kept my fears to myself and no one in the house knew what I was going through. I didn't want to scare them and trusted that God would heal whatever was in my body without placing a burden on anyone.

Sometime in late 2004 the combination of headaches, fever and fatigue had become almost unbearable, so my cousin took me to the doctor. As I entered the doctor's office I had a panic attack and was fearful of what the doctor would find as she started to examine my body. "Miss Consolee, have you ever been tested for HIV?" she immediately asked.

I had been dreading that question for a long time and it hit me like a bolt of lightning, but I had reached the point where there was no turning back. "No . . . No, doctor, I . . . I have never been tested," I replied, almost whispering.

"Don't be scared my dear, I just want to make sure that you are okay so I have to test you for everything," she replied calmly. Her response gave me some psychological relief which was interrupted when she said: "If you find out that you're HIV positive, don't worry you will get proper medication that will clear all those marks on your body, and you will live longer."

As my cousin and I drove back home to await the results, a coldness developed within me which never left me for that entire week. The results came back the following week and the doctor contacted me by phone. "Miss Consolee, I'm sorry I have bad news. Unfortunately, your results show that you are HIV positive, but you should not worry as there is medication available that will help you to live an almost normal life."

Luckily I was at home at the time, for had I been on the street God alone knows what could have befallen me! That news was so devastating to me that I couldn't find any words to speak and my head became as light as a feather. I just sat there trying to process what she had told me, and at the same time thinking about the impact that such a sickness would have on me.

After giving me some time to compose myself, the doctor again spoke. "You can go to the Nassau University Medical Center where you will get treatment!" I was still in a daze and all I was able to say was 'goodbye' to the doctor. Luckily my cousin Chantal and a friend

Concessa were at home and they observed the dramatic change in my countenance.

"Consolee, are you okay? Who was that on the phone and what did they tell you?" Chantal asked with concern. I broke down in tears and started shaking uncontrollably and the two of them came close to me and embraced me, still asking me to tell them what was happening. It took me some time before I could speak and I finally was able to share the bad news with them.

After taking a few hours to calm myself, Chantal and Concessa took me to the hospital and they were later joined by my cousin, her husband and Concessa's husband. It was very emotional and shocking to all of them and they cried openly as they saw me lying scared and worried on that hospital bed. As for me I was already numb and didn't have any words to express how I felt.

While at the hospital a nurse brought a hospital gown and told me I have to wear it. I was so fragile at the time that this simple gesture crushed my spirit and I started to cry incessantly, thinking that I was about to die. "God, please help me to be strong!" I pleaded as I prayed passionately to God. The reality of being on that hospital bed brought back painful memories of how I was raped and reminded me that it was the cause of me lying there with that illness.

"You will be okay Consolee; don't worry, we are here for you!" echoed Chantal, Immaculee and Bryan with tears also streaming down their faces. It was very painful to all of them and they couldn't contain their tears whenever they turned their eyes to look at me.

"Be strong, Consolee, we will be back to see you tomorrow and will be praying for you!" they said to me as they hugged me and said goodbye. That night I couldn't sleep as a multitude of thoughts flooded my mind. "How am I going to live knowing that I am HIV positive? How are my friends and family going to treat me after knowing about my illness?" I kept asking myself.

Those were questions that I didn't know how to answer, as I knew that many people were afraid of being around persons living with HIV/AIDS. What gave me consolation was the fact that those closest to me were compassionate and sad when they learned about my condition, and were not shunning me in any way. I did not sleep a wink that night as I was reading my bible, meditating and praying to God constantly to keep me strong and help me maintain my sanity. I got some relief from the meditation and felt a little peaceful within, and the nurses kept coming back and forth to check on me in my room. They were very nice talking to me, asking me how I felt and reassuring me that I would be okay. I thank God that I met caring nurses on duty that night.

The following day I received a telephone call from a special person Dr. Wayne Dyer, a very close friend of the family who was able to lift my spirit with his kind and compassionate words of wisdom. "Consolee my dear; do not worry and continue to think positively. You have to believe that you will be healed, and should never think for one moment that you will not be!" he said to me soothingly. "Please write down my telephone number, and you can call me anytime whenever you need to talk to me!" he added at the end of his call.

Dr. Dyer's comforting and uplifting words strengthened me and gave me hope during that very sensitive period. His call was very fatherly and it put me at ease, and I felt like my father's spirit was being channeled through him.

Later that day, a Social Worker was assigned to help me with information relating to the treatment process. She was very compassionate and kind to me in every word that she expressed, and provided me with all the information I needed to know. She also gave me some spiritual booklets and other literature to read, which lifted my spirits and gave me strength. I was very happy and was thanking God for sending me those wonderful people to help me through that critical period of my life.

That night I felt motivated to turn on the TV and watch one of my favorite shows, OPRAH. Coincidentally, the episode that day focused on people who had a positive approach to life despite difficulties they had endured, and it inspired me to follow their lead. I slept well that night and it was the first time I was able to sleep since hearing the news of my diagnosis.

I was still fragile about my newly confirmed HIV status and had to keep telling myself that I will be fine and that I have to show it outwardly. It was not easy but I kept reminding myself that there must be a purpose for all that had happened to me, but I just did not know what it was as yet. I wanted to have a positive outlook upon my return to my job, and wasn't ready to share my health status with anyone else except family members as yet.

While there at the hospital, my cousin called and said to me: "Consolee, I just spoke to Judith Garten who asked about you. I told her that you're sick but she insisted that she wants to speak to you." I responded that it was not a problem, so it was okay to give Judith my number.

My phone rang later that day and when I answered it was Judith at the other end. "Consolee dear, I heard that you're sick and I want to come to visit you. What would you like me to get for you?" she asked in a loving way.

"I would like an inspirational book," I replied.

"Great! I know a wonderful author who could inspire you!" she responded cheerfully.

I was very happy that Judith would be coming to see me because we had become very close. She is a very good friend of ours and cared for all of us in the family. The next day, Judith came all the way from Woodstock and told me that she couldn't wait to come and see me when she heard I wasn't feeling well. We spoke and I told her what I was diagnosed with and she comforted me as she was used to doing in the past. She reminded me of her promise to bring me an inspirational book, and smiled as she rummaged through her bag searching for it.

"This woman is a wonderful author, you will like her" she said, as she pulled out the book and a chain she had brought for me. "Oh, thank you so much, Judith, you are so kind!" I said as I observed the title of the book 'A return to love' by Marianne Williamson.

Judith spent some time with me talking and consoling me before she left. I was very thrilled that she came and showed me her good heart, and thanked her so much for doing so. After she left I started reading the book and couldn't put it down. It was very inspiring and it calmed and comforted me in so many ways. I started feeling a little confident within myself and I fell in love with everything the author had written in that book.

I think that God never allowed any disturbances within my heart while I was in that hospital. Accepting my new health status was going to tear me apart if I didn't get comfort from the people I interacted with during my time there. Their comfort allowed me to have a moment to begin to accept my illness and learn a little about being more trusting in God. I felt that I was chosen to carry the burden of that illness and was prepared to accept such sacrifice as God's will in my life, which I saw as the beginning of my healing process. I started to ask Him to help me cope after I leave the hospital so that I can keep reinforcing the positive thinking within me.

On the last day of my stay at the hospital the doctor came in to my room with a smile on his face. "I have good news for you Miss. Nishimwe! You will be leaving this afternoon and will need to return as an outpatient for follow up visits! You are on the road to recovery and I wish you good luck!" he said to me.

I went home feeling a great deal better than I felt when the HIV diagnosis was first confirmed to me. Of course I was still fragile and it was easy for me to get upset about simple things, but I had to think again that I have to return to work and would need to be normal with my coworkers to avoid making it obvious that something so drastic had happened to me.

I was going to start medication soon and was not sure how it was going to affect my daily life, but in any event I had to be conscious and not show any signs because of the stigma surrounding people suffering with HIV. I also knew that my lifestyle would have to be changed and there was so much going on through my head and I did not have a clue about how I would handle those changes. I still needed a lot of time to talk to a professional counselor to help me deal with my emotional situation and I tried to help myself by pleading with God in my daily prayers to help me feel and act normal.

I also thought that I had to find the right time and environment to call my mother and tell her about it, but I needed some time to relax my brain before I could have the courage to tell her. Something like this could never be an easy thing to tell to a mother, but I felt she needed to know. This was something that would break her heart again but I trusted that she would "take it in stride" knowing the many horrors she had bravely faced and overcome during the genocide, which my current situation could hardly compare with.

When I felt I was ready, I got up one morning and decided that after saying my prayers I would talk to my mom. I relaxed myself, picked up the phone, and called her. We talked and laughed at the beginning as usual and after a while I paused a bit and told her: "Mama, do you remember the bumps I was developing on my skin before I left? I went to the doctor recently to find out about them and to get treated and she asked me to take a HIV test. I took the test and the results showed that I am HIV positive!"

We both immediately started to cry, and amid the avalanche of tears Mom quickly said to me: "My child, don't worry about anything; it is God who rescued you from the horrible genocide and he will continue to protect you and keep you strong and healthy. You will be okay!" and quickly added: "I love you my child. Be strong and pray more!" to which I replied: "I love you Mom, and I can't imagine what I would have done if I didn't have you!"

I was still crying but somewhat relieved in my heart that Mom was there to comfort me, and was touched by the way her voice conveyed such true affection. It was not an easy conversation for us, but to avoid having it was not an option for me.

As soon as we finished talking that day Mom sent me a text message saying: "Be strong ma Cherie, I know our God will be with my baby because you are the greatest joy He has put into my life!" That text made me cry again with joy and I thanked God for having rescued my wonderful Mom to be there to show love and affection and to comfort me in my critical moments of anguish. "I thank God, Mama Cherie to have you in my life! I will be strong because of you and I love you so much Mama!" I replied to her by text message.

I continued to cry a bit after that exchange and when I had finished I sat down and imagined the state she was in back there at home in Rwanda. I said a prayer and asked of God: "O Lord, please keep my mother strong. She has been through a lot herself, so don't let her lose hope! Make her know that you will perform miracles in her child's life!"

From that day onwards Mom kept checking on me through text messages with words of comfort and so much love that soothed and strengthened me. When I think of the many other women who went through the same or even worse than I did, and through no fault of their own did not have the family support to help them deal with their emotional pain, it strikes at the core of my heart.

After leaving the hospital, I stayed at home for three days and used that time to exercise my inner self and test whether I was ready to face my coworkers and maintain the same outlook and motivation I had before I left. They knew me as a pleasant person who naturally smiles a lot, and luckily for me, that did not change despite my new situation. Of course, when I was alone I couldn't help but cry sometimes and ask God to help me deal with the pain, but in public I handled my emotions pretty well. Thankfully, after returning to work there was not even a single day that I felt really sick, and nothing was showing on my body that could make a person suspicious of my illness. I didn't want to go through the added pain of being discriminated against or stigmatized by anyone because of my condition.

On the day I returned to work, of course my colleagues asked me how I was feeling. I told them that I was feeling fine, and provided the director with a doctor's note. I did my work in the way I was accustomed to and tried my best to conceal the emotional conflicts that were going on inside me. I didn't want to hurt anyone or attract bad attitudes towards me as a result of them becoming privy to my health status, so most of the time I dealt with my emotional pain when I was on my break time by silently crying to myself or scribbling on paper whatever I was feeling at the moment.

Two weeks later I went back to the clinic for a follow up visit and to receive my medication. I was already told by the hospital who my nurse practitioner would be and which doctor was assigned to me. I was introduced to my nurse practitioner Patricia, who appeared warm and friendly and greeted me as such. "You will be fine Consolee, we will take very good care of you!" she said to me.

Patricia contacted the doctor who she was teaming up with to work on my care, and he came to her office shortly after, looked at me, smiled, and said "miracles do happen!" Hearing him as a doctor say that gave me added hope and I told myself "God is great, who knows what could happen to me?" I believed it during the genocide in my country, I believed it when the doctor said it to me, and I still believe today, that miracles do happen and they do happen through God's power.

Patricia and the doctor did everything that was expected of them, explained the "do's and don'ts" associated with the medication and the illness, and also gave me lessons on how to maintain a healthy lifestyle by eating well and exercising frequently. I listened carefully because I wanted to live well and longer, and to be in a position to advise and encourage others who might take it lightly or didn't care about their life anymore because of having the illness.

I was really grateful that Patricia put me on the right path and assured me that she would be there for me in any way she could. As time went by, I kept up with my outpatient appointments at the clinic and was definitely happy to see the improvement that was taking place in my body. Every time I went they would tell me how great I looked and that my readings were showing well, and I felt reassured every time.

★   ★   ★

REFLECTIONS ON CHAPTER 17

Every person who had an input in providing me support, solace and medical care during that initial period of my diagnosis with HIV showed extreme sympathy, love and consciousness for my frailty. This served as the cornerstone for my manageable acceptance of my condition.

I must extend my deep and heartfelt thanks to the professionals at the hospital, my family and friends for reaching out to me in the way they did. It is people like those who put a human face and heart in their interaction with others, or to the jobs that they do, who truly make the difference between a person in my situation either adjusting positively to their newly discovered HIV status, or degenerating to self pity and absolute loss of motivation for life.

In this life here on earth there is no better way of bringing joy and harmony to your heart and soul than being kind to others, to help whoever you can, and to empathize from the heart with those less fortunate than you are. Sometimes we say to ourselves that we don't have much to offer, but I believe that simply giving love from your heart and a caring smile to the downtrodden is enough to show that you care.

CHAPTER 18

FINDING HOPE

During my short lifetime, I have experienced so many dreadful things that have hurt me so badly and made me feel that life is so difficult to live. When I looked around after the genocide I had to face the grim reality that I had lost so many people who mattered most in my life, contracted HIV as a result of the atrocities that were forced upon me, and now had to spend the rest of my life enduring the emotional pain associated with all those tragic circumstances. Even though I was fortunate that a few of my closest family members survived, I still suffered so many deep pains as a young girl, with my only consolation being the fact that so many other survivors were going through the same things like me. Those pains were very deep seated and disruptive to any feelings of well being that ventured to surface within me.

My everyday life was a constant struggle and I cried myself to sleep many nights in the privacy of my bed, not wanting to show the pain I was going through. I could not shake off the feeling of shame that constantly engulfed my inner being whenever I thought about the sexual violence I had suffered, and always saw myself as abnormal and different to other girls my age who did not suffer that type of misfortune.

As the years slowly went by, I gradually started to replace my feelings of despair with thoughts that I still had *life* so I should therefore still have *hope*, and began to convince myself that God is still there for me so I should focus on his power and pray for his healing and guidance, instead of dwelling on my pain. I started praying incessantly, telling God everything that was in my heart. Those moments of deep prayer and meditation started to lift up my spirit, and over time I started to surround myself with people who complemented those uplifting moments with their positive outlook and energy. I also tried to help myself by reading uplifting books and other inspirational forms of literature, and that combination brought about some semblance of inner peace and a firm reassurance that my life mattered after all.

I remember it was around the summer of 1999 when I started telling myself that I survived the horror of the genocide for a reason through God's grace, and that he has a purpose for extending my life here on earth despite the turmoil I had faced. This helped me to feel that each day is a treasure that I need to embrace and be grateful for, as many others were not as fortunate as I am. It also gave me the consciousness of thought that none of us are in control of our destiny, and we must be grateful for whatever mercy comes our way, no matter how small it may seem in our eyes. We are all precious in God's eyes, but he has different plans for each and every one of us. Such acceptance and my surrender to God's will in my life set the stage for the beginning of my psychological progress, and today I feel hopeful that I can face whatever new challenges come my way. I do my best to avoid harboring any ill feelings within me, as I know that such ill feelings about my self or anyone else will ultimately become a poison to my soul.

It took me more than 15 years to decide to write about my experiences during the genocide, as the effect it had on me had continued to cloud my aspirations and erode my beliefs that I could still accomplish the big goals I had before it started. I was also fearful that I would offend those who were responsible, even though I would be stating facts about the unimaginable horrors we had faced for decades as a Tutsi minority in my beloved country, which climaxed into that infamous period of ethnic cleansing in 1994.

Today, I have found the hope and courage to pursue the big goals and dreams I had back then, and more importantly, have cast aside the fear that by speaking the truth I would offend those who had offended me, and am therefore no longer afraid to state the horrific facts about what we faced as a people in 1994.

The hope I have found is also rooted in the rapid strides Rwanda has made in educating our "blinded countrymen" about the merits of coexisting peacefully as Rwandans, and eradicating the use of divisive systems that only serve to create distinctions and cause divisions between the different ethnic groups of our beloved country. Rwanda has risen majestically out of the ashes, due in great measure to the renewed opportunities for education of the people and their determination to chart a better future for themselves and ensure that the precious blood of their loved ones whose lives were lost would not have been sacrificed in vain.

The government and people of Rwanda must be highly credited for their commitment and vision for bringing us as a people closer together in such a record period of time, and against the backdrop of such insurmountable mayhem that destroyed the physical and moral fabric of our society. I am encouraged by what I have seen accomplished over the past 18 years, which has drastically improved the quality of life of our people and transformed the highly negative stigma the genocide placed on Rwanda as a country, into a nation that can be considered as a model of success for poor developing countries like itself.

★　★　★

REFLECTIONS ON CHAPTER 18

I used to have so many wonderful people among my family and friends who used to enjoy the beauty of our homeland with me. I always looked forward to them being around for me in that beautiful land God has created for all of us, but most of those people were taken away in a flash during the 1994 genocide, taking my dreams with them.

No matter our circumstances, we as human beings hope and aspire to live a blissful life, having people around us to show love and care for one another and enjoy what God has created for us in peace and harmony. When a tragedy as extreme as Genocide occurs, you lose the focus of those aspirations and your will and confidence are broken.

My lesson to all is that no matter what horrible circumstances we may face in our lives, we must never lose hope, for losing hope is the beginning of our own self defeat.

Relaxing with friends in the summer of 1996, two years after the genocide. I'm second from the right, with my friend Laetitia to my left and sister Jeanette and cousin Chantal to my right.

My friend Rebecca (stooping) and I, in traditional Rwandese dress in 2000.

My sister Jeanette in 2004 at age 22.

Mom's cousin Sister Agnes in her habit in Rwanda in 2006.

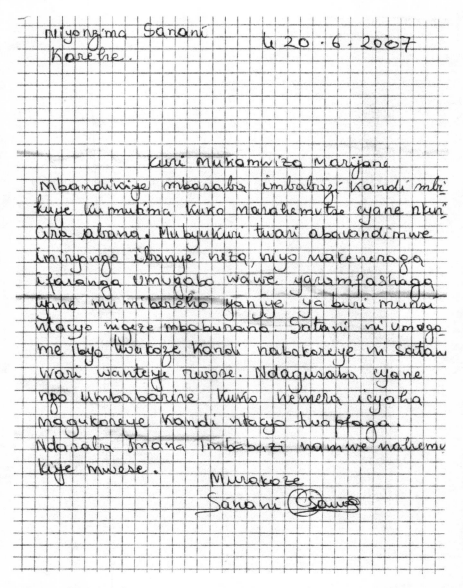

niyongima Sanani   4 20.6.2007
Karehe.

        Kuri Mukamwiza Marijane
Mbandikiye mbasaba imbabazi. Kandi mbi
kuye ku mutima kuko marahemutse cyane nkuri
aba abana. Mubyukuri twari abavandimwe
iminyango ibanye neza, niyo makeneraga
ifaranga umugabo wawe yarampashaga
kane mu miberebo yanje ya buri munsi
ntacyo nacze mbabunana. Satani ni umugo
me ibyo twakoze Kandi nababareye ni Satani
wari wanteye ruvoze. Ndagusaba cyane
ngo umbabarine kuko nemera icyaha
magukoreye kandi ntacyo twaftaga.
Ndasaba Imana Imbabazi namwe nahemu
kiye mwese.
                Murakoze
                Sanani

Copy of Sanani's letter to my mom in 2007 asking for her forgiveness for
killing my three young brothers.

My mom during the burial ceremony of my three brothers in 2009.

My cousin Chantal and I at an event in California USA, in 2010.

Sandra in 2011 (now fully grown) who had suffered chop wounds to her head during the genocide.

EPILOGUE

Some Justice, Some Closure

One of the most difficult issues which my family struggled to come to terms with after the genocide was trying to comprehend how could it have been possible for our very close neighbors Sanani, Shinani and Jackson among others, to betray the decades of kindness and friendship we had shown them and become so vicious towards us. A contrasting difficulty which compounded our pain was the fact that Damas, my dad's killer, did not know my dad prior to the time of his murder, and it felt so unfair to us that his precious life was snuffed out by this man without reason.

For years following the genocide, my mom grappled with these issues, having to balance her severe emotional pain with her principles of resisting hatred and revenge against those who had hurt us. Over time, her renewed friendship with Sanani's sister Christine continued to grow and their friendship with each other is still ongoing up to today. As the years passed, Sanani's father and other members of his wider family circle had been visiting my mother to express their remorse, and the previously close relationship which our family had shared with theirs slowly began to rekindle.

In 2011 Sanani's father passed away and shortly before his death he encouraged his family to maintain the friendship they had re-developed with my family, and asked that one of his cows be given to my mother as a symbol of that friendship. Upon his death, his family honored his wishes and presented my mother with the cow which she accepted in good faith.

As for Sanani, he continues to pay the price for the killing of my innocent baby brothers and is currently in prison serving life sentences for the many killings he had committed during the genocide.

In the case of Shinani, he was imprisoned for crimes he had committed against me and others during the genocide, and died in prison in the year 2000. Today, only two of his family members reside in the area, one brother who occupies the family home situated across from where we lived, and another who lives a short distance away.

Jackson, our closest neighbor, unceremoniously fled Rwanda when the country was liberated in July 1994 and his current fate or whereabouts are unknown.

It took over thirteen years for me and my family to see the killer of my brothers face justice for their murders. Sanani's public apology and subsequent lifetime imprisonment in 2007, together with my mother's eventual courage to retrieve my brothers' remains and give them a proper burial in 2009 has helped to bring us some closure.

Shinani's death in prison six years after committing those horrible acts against me and others denied us the chance of seeing him face justice here on earth, but nevertheless, I carry no burden in my heart as I am certain that he has already answered to God's justice. The fact that I had put his fate in the hands of God even before his passing served to bring me personal closure.

As for Damas, my Dad's killer, he was imprisoned for many years and later tried in GACACA Court for his murder. He eventually confessed to my dad's killing and threw himself at the mercy of the court. The court took into consideration Damas' confession and the fact that he had already served many years in prison, and in 2008 he was released and ordered to perform community service.

Given the scale and severity of what we had endured both as individuals and as a family, it would be reasonable to say that the levels of justice and closure we have received to date appear miniscule when compared with those that are still unresolved.

It is painful to live with the knowledge that the remains of my father, grandparents and multiple other members of my family were never found and the killers of many of them have not been brought to justice. Nevertheless, I remain firm in my belief that God has already rewarded their sacrifice and has accepted them into his heavenly kingdom. That belief has provided me with the satisfaction and closure I need, and encourages me to continue to live my life with faith, hope and enthusiasm.

ACKNOWLEDGEMENTS

I would like to thank God for showering me with his divine protection during the genocide and for giving me the strength and courage to write this book. I would also like to thank each and everyone who have contributed in any way to its creation, and especially:

★ My mother Marie Jeanne Mukamwiza for providing background information on many past events relating to members of our family and life in Rwanda as they were growing up, and for being our pillar of strength through all the adversities that we faced during the actual genocide in 1994 and in its aftermath. She is the most loving mother one could ever wish for and I feel blessed to have her as my mother.

★ My aunt Esperance Mukarugaba for being supportive of my efforts to tell my story and for also providing me with information about the history of our family life in Kibuye. She has been a constant source of encouragement and inspiration to me during my struggles after the genocide, and I consider her as a friend as well as an aunt who I love so much and to whom I am deeply grateful.

★ My sister Jeanette Ingabire for all her encouragement and support for the documentation of our experiences and the love she has always shown me. She has shared my pain despite her own fragile circumstances and I truly admire and appreciate the strength she showed in overcoming the difficult traumas in her own life. She is so full of love and understanding and cares for me as much as I do her.

★ My cousin Chantal Nyirarukundo for being a great "sister" to me and for her love, care and affection before, during and after our tumultuous period in 1994. She has been a consistent source of encouragement and motivation to me and has helped me overcome some of the deep traumas I faced in my life and supported me greatly in this venture to document our experiences. I truly love her for who she is.

★ Dr. Wayne Dyer for his kindness and the support he has given me, and his motivational advice and encouragement to tell my story. He is truly a godsend and I can never thank him enough for his good heart and commitment to teach the world the benefits of remaining "in spirit."

★ Elizabeth Swart for the love and personal attention she has shown me from the very first time we met, and the constant communication she maintains and the care she continues to freely provide me. She has been like a mother to me and has motivated me to reach for higher heights, which helped me greatly in making my decision to write this book. She is a true friend and one whom I am grateful to have in my life.

★ Bryan Black for his extreme dedication and competence in editing my manuscript and for his valuable inputs and guidance throughout the course of its documentation. He has converted my raw story into one that is truly reader-friendly and has brought my experiences back to life. I am deeply grateful to him for his professional inputs and innovative insights.

★ Gabrielle Bernstein for her spiritual support and encouragement through her daily teachings and personal interaction with me. She is my great friend and spiritual sister.

★ Judith Garten for her love, care and support especially during my fragile period in hospital. I can always count on her for advice and inspiration whenever I feel down. She is my true friend and counselor.

★ Francine Lefrak for her continuous warmth and friendliness towards me, and her support, guidance and sage advice in the preparation of my manuscript. Her ideas helped me to better express some of the deep-seated emotions I had experienced as a 14 year old girl during the genocide. I am grateful for the hope and support she provides to HIV-positive women survivors in Rwanda through her Same Sky Initiative.

★ To my Rwandese friends and fellow survivors in New York and New Jersey who meet with me regularly to exchange ideas about helping other survivors and to listen to each other and provide support as needed. I am grateful that we are all in each other's lives.

★ To all my fellow survivors in Rwanda and other parts of the world for their strength, courage and perseverance despite the challenges that we all face. Don't give up on your aspirations and know that you are loved and constantly in my prayers.

★ To all my friends and relatives, too numerous to mention, who have encouraged and assisted me in different ways in the course of my writing of this book.

ABOUT THE AUTHOR

Consolee Nishimwe is a survivor of the 1994 genocide against Tutsis in Rwanda. Born in Western Province, she lived through the horrors of genocide at age 14. She was at her home in Rubengera, Kibuye with her parents and four siblings when the genocide started on April 6, and they were forced to leave their home and go into hiding. Unfortunately, her father and three young brothers were murdered along with many other close relatives. Consolee suffered physical torture during her three months in hiding, and miraculously survived with her mother and younger sister. She is a committed speaker on the genocide and an advocate for the survivors who suffered physical and emotional torture. She is also a defender of global women's rights.

GLOSSARY

A wheat and a leaf green: Rwandese proverb meaning "knowing right from wrong"

Cherie: French word meaning "dear"

Commune: District.

GACACA: Traditional court system.

Hutu: Largest ethnic group of Rwanda

Inkotanyi: Kinyarwanda word meaning "fierce warrior"

Interahamwe Extremely ruthless militia group affiliated with the previous government's political party, MRND

Inyenzi: Kinyarwanda word meaning "cockroach"

Ma Cherie French term meaning "my dear"

Macwa: Author's nickname

Ma Fille Cherie: French term meaning "my dear daughter"

Musazi: Kinyarwanda word meaning "fool"

Ntampongano Y'umwanzi: Kinyarwanda phrase meaning "no pity for our enemies."

Sector: County.

Tutsi: Second largest ethnic group of Rwanda

Twa: Smallest ethnic group of Rwanda

RESOURCES

IBUKA Association of Genocide Survivors
   http://www.ibuka.rw

Same Sky Trade-not-Aid Initiative
   http://www.samesky.com/

Genocide Survivors Support Network
   http://www.genocidesurvivorssupportnetwork.org/

Miracle Corners of the World
   http://www.miraclecorners.org/jacquelines_human_rights_
   corner.htm

CPSIA information can be obtained
at www.ICGtesting.com
Printed in the USA
JSHW061237170822
29395JS00001B/92